THE MAKING OF THE ENGLISH LANDSCAPE

THE BEDFORDSHIRE AND HUNTINGDONSHIRE LANDSCAPE

THE MAKING OF THE ENGLISH LANDSCAPE
Edited by W. G. Hoskins and Roy Millward

THE MAKING OF THE WELSH LANDSCAPE
Edited by W. G. Hoskins and Roy Millward

The Bedfordshire and Huntingdonshire Landscape

by

PETER BIGMORE

HODDER AND STOUGHTON
LONDON SYDNEY AUCKLAND TORONTO

British Library Cataloguing in Publication Data

Bigmore, Peter
  The Bedfordshire and Huntingdonshire
  landscape.—(Making of the English landscape).
  1. Bedfordshire, Eng.—Historical geography
  2. Huntingdonshire, Eng.—Historical geography
  I. Title   II. Series
  911'.425'6   DA670.B3

ISBN 0–340–24149–7

To Madeleine

Preface

ANYONE who attempts to cover in one book the dual
aspects of landscape and history, and for two counties, is
almost invariably faced with the problem of what to leave
out. I have not devoted much space, therefore, to dealing
with those aspects of the landscape that are to be readily
found discussed elsewhere, such as the finer points of the
architecture of great houses and churches or the attractiveness of certain villages and places, concentrating instead
upon those features that best illustrate the themes of colonisation and settlement, of agriculture and industry. There
are some who will regard an emphasis on archaeological
information as providing a cold, almost clinical approach
to the two counties and who will look for the personalities
that have given flesh to the local history. But it is not this
book's purpose to provide a social history such as already
exists, at least in part, for Bedfordshire and Huntingdonshire, and it is to the skills of the archaeologist and aerial
photographer that I owe my first debt in the way that they
have widened my conceptions of the landscape history.

Presented with such a wide range of material, of documents, maps, photographs and the excavated artefacts of
past communities I am conscious of my inexpertise in
interpreting all of them, and of the value of those who have
passed on their years of experience to me. Some of them
have done so unknowingly and it is appropriate that I record
my gratitude to them here. Joyce Godber's excellent *History
of Bedfordshire* is a mine of information, a most valuable
introduction to the local history of the county, culled from
her many years as County Archivist. In Huntingdonshire
another former archivist, Philip Dickinson, has taken his
deep interest in topographic history far enough to leave the
Record Office with a collection of manuscript maps and

documents, all prepared with an eye for meticulous detail. Bedfordshire owes another debt of gratitude to the late Dr Herbert Fowler, whose many interests are not only to be found in the articles he contributed to the Bedfordshire Historical Record Society but also in the library he left to the county which is now in the care of the Bedfordshire Library Service at County Hall. His collection of published State Papers and local histories must rank as one of the finest to be found in the provinces.

In my frequent use of the Record Offices at Bedford and Huntingdon the staff could not have been more helpful with their comments and their ability to produce documents of which I had been woefully ignorant. I thank particularly Patricia Bell, Archivist at Bedford, and Miss Thomas and Mrs Mackey at Huntingdon for their assistance in photographing a number of maps and prints. David Baker, Conservation Officer for Bedfordshire, kindly allowed me to use the County Sites and Monuments Record and corrected some of the misconceptions I had formed over the distribution of archaeological sites, although my conclusions remain my own.

There are those I must thank for making my work easier in other ways. Steve Chilton of the Middlesex Polytechnic Cartographic Unit provided valuable assistance with taking and reproducing some of the photographs, and if the Polytechnic had not allowed me a term's sabbatical leave in the Autumn of 1977 I doubt if the book could have been finished within any reasonable length of time. I am also grateful to my colleague, Dr Eric Grant, for his helpful advice and for undertaking my teaching during my absence. Finally, I must thank Roy Millward, whose teaching some years ago first set me on the path of local history and whose editorial advice has considerably improved the original manuscript.

PETER BIGMORE

1979

Contents

List of Plates

Acknowledgments

The author wishes to thank the following for permission to reproduce their photographs and documents:

The Committee for Aerial Photography, Cambridge: Plates 1, 2, 5, 7, 8, 9, 12, 13 (photographs by Professor J. K. St Joseph, Cambridge University Collection: copyright reserved).
Aerofilms Limited: Plates 10, 11, 18, 39, 40 (copyright reserved).
The Trustees of the Bedford Estates: Plate 6 (copyright reserved).
The Right Hon. Lady Lucas: Plates 19 and 20 (copyright reserved).
The remainder of the plates are the copyright of the author.

List of maps and plans

Editor's Introduction

THIS SERIES OF books on The Making of the English Landscape originated in 1955 with my own pioneer book under that title. A few county volumes were published under the same format (Cornwall, Leicestershire, Gloucestershire, and Lancashire), but a new and better format was worked out from 1970 onwards, beginning with Arthur Raistrick's *West Riding of Yorkshire* and Christopher Taylor's *Dorset*. Since then there has been a steady flow of such county studies, aiming at covering the whole country eventually. Already there have been volumes as far apart as Northumberland and Sussex; and books are in preparation ranging from Kent in the east to a revised edition of Cornwall in the far west.

Purists might object that the geographical county has no particular unity except for administrative purposes, that the 'region' would be more appropriate. Apart from the fact that few would agree about what constituted a 'region', the primary fact is that the geographical county is a unity so far as the documentary material is concerned; but, more than that, it evokes local patriotism, and again each English county (one ought to say 'British' in view of the fact that Wales has been brought within the orbit of the series) contains a wide variety of landscapes each interesting and appealing in its own right. Every county presents a multitude of problems of Landscape History and their very contrast is illuminating. Even little Rutland has such contrasts, though naturally on a more limited scale; and a large county like Devon has almost every kind of landscape. One other point: when the reorganisation of local government took place a few years ago, and some entirely new names appeared on the administrative map of England, such as Avon and Cleveland, I had to consider whether we should stick to the old counties as we have always known them or adopt the new set-up. As the series was by then so far advanced under the old and well-loved names, we decided to retain them and go on as before. There were other good reasons, besides the senti-mental one, for sticking to the original plan.

It is a well-worn truism that England is a very small country with an almost infinite variety of rocks, soils, topo-graphy, and watercourses by the tens of thousands: all these things create what one might call micro-landscapes at the risk of importing a little professional jargon into something which is meant to be enjoyed and explained in plain English. One look at the coloured map of the geology of England and Wales and above all the way in which the colours change every few miles, is enough to excite the visual imagination. This is especially true when one crosses the grain of a piece of country, instead of travelling along it. There is for example the major grain, so to speak, which runs from the south-west coast in Dorset north-eastwards to the Yorkshire coast round Whitby. If you cut *across* this geological grain, going from south-east to north-west the landscapes change every few miles. On a smaller scale but nearly as complicated, the south-eastern corner of England, running from say New-haven northwards to the Thames estuary, presents rapid and very contrasted changes of landscape—in soils, building stones (and hence buildings themselves), in vernacular building—the architectural equivalent of the once-rich variety of local dialects in this country—in land-forms, in farming, in almost everything that is visible.

Most of us enjoy some widespread view from a hilltop or on some grand coast: we enjoy it as 'scenery' but this is really a superficial enjoyment. What I prefer to call 'land-scape' as distinct from 'scenery' is that a landscape to me asks questions: why is something like this at all, why does it differ from another view a few miles away? It is the difference perhaps between what an amateur portrait painter sees and puts on paper and what a skilled surgeon sees when he contemplates and reflects over a human body. He sees things, even on a superficial examination, because of his training and his long experience, that the layman never sees. So it is with *landscape*. To see it thus, seeing beneath the surface and the obvious, is to increase one's enjoyment of the English countryside enormously. The great English painter John Constable makes this point in one simple sentence in one of his *Discourses on Landscape,* a sentence I shall never tire of quoting: "*We see nothing till we truly understand it.*" Constable's *Discourses* were an attempt to justify landscape-painting as an end in itself. If we take his great dictum as our text, Landscape History becomes an end in itself, transmuting the textbook facts of rocks and soils, landforms, economic history, industrial archaeology—words calculated to deter all but the most determined reader—into a different way of looking at perhaps commonplace things, into a different language. The art is to use these academic disciplines in a concealed way, never to let them obtrude or, if so, to some essential purpose so that the visual is always paramount.

When I wrote my own book now more than twenty years ago I did not answer all the possible questions by a long way, though it still stands as a good introduction to a new field of history. Landscape History is now, I think, a well-accepted and respectable discipline, taught in some universities and in schools, and the subject of theses. I did not answer all the questions for the simple reason that I did not then know what they all were. And even now, after so many books and articles and theses have been written, there is so much that remains unknown, and no doubt questions that I, and others, have still not perceived. This, to me, is one of the great values of these landscape books, treated county by county. Local studies in depth, to use a fashionable phrase, but for once a useful one, will not only enlarge our generalisations about the major changes in the landscape, but also because of their detail bring new lights into the picture. Ideally, as editor of this series, I would like each writer on a particular county to pick out an even smaller area for special examination under the microscope, having in mind such revealing studies as Professor Harry Thorpe's masterly essay on Wormleighton in Warwickshire (*The Lord and the Landscape,* published in 1965) and Dr Jack Ravensdale's *Liable to Floods* (1974) which deals with three Fen-Edge villages in Cambridgeshire. Not only are the topographical settings of these two studies so completely different, but one is concerned with 'peasant villages' and the landscapes they created. So social structure also enters into the many hidden creators of a particular bit of England and the vision it presents.

Some major problems remain virtually unsolved. I myself in my first book fell into the trap, or rather accepted the current doctrine, that until the Old English Conquest most of this country was uncleared woodland or undrained marsh or in many parts primeval moorland. To a large extent I was deceived by the overwhelming evidence of the number of Old English place-names on the map, or, if not these, then the powerful Scandinavian element in the eastern parts of England. I am no longer deceived, or perhaps I should say that I have become much more sceptical about the ultimate value of this treacherous evidence. Thanks to archaeological advances in the past twenty years (and partly thanks to the opportunities offered by the odious onwards march of the motorways—their only value in my eyes) we know very much more about the density of settlement and of population in prehistoric times right back to the Mesolithic of seven or eight thousand years ago. There is evidence for forest clearance and to some extent for settled farming as early as this, and to an even greater extent by Neolithic times when one thinks of the axe-factories two thousand or more feet up on the wildest mountains of Lakeland. Forest clearance was going on at this height, and axes were being exported as far south as the coast of Hampshire. We now need a completely fresh study of the distribution of woodland by, say, Romano-British times. Not only woodland clearance, but the river gravels which have been exploited by modern man for his new roads have changed our whole concept of prehistoric settlement. The gravels of the Welland valley, almost in the heart of the Midlands, have been particularly intensively studied and have changed our entire thinking in these parts.

That is one aspect of the English landscape which I greatly under-estimated when I first wrote and I welcome every fresh piece of evidence that proves me misguided. Yet all the same the outlines of the main picture remain unchanged, and I stand by that first book subject to such changes of emphasis as I have mentioned.

There are other problems waiting to be worked out, some special to particular bits of England, others of a more general nature. Of the special problems I think of the number of isolated parish churches in the beautiful county of Norfolk: why are they there, stuck out all alone in the fields? Somebody could write a wonderful book on Churches in the Landscape. And there are other special aspects of the landscape wherever one walks in this most beloved of all countries: so much to do, so little done. These closer studies of England county by county will add enormously to our knowledge. Already the study of Landscape History has attracted a growing literature of its own, a great deal of it scattered in local journals and periodicals. Soon, perhaps in ten years' time, we shall need a Bibliography of the subject. This makes it sound dull and academic, but in the end I look upon it as an enlargement of consciousness, a new way of looking at familiar scenes which adds to the enjoyment of life. For those who have eyes to see, the face of Britain will never look the same again.

Exeter, 1976   W. G. HOSKINS

1. The early settlers

The natural landscape. Prehistoric settlers. The Roman intrusion.

The natural landscape

THE CHARMS of Bedfordshire and Huntingdonshire draw few visitors from beyond their boundaries and yet the number of people who pass through, by road or rail, must be as great as for any other county within the southern half of England. The two counties lie astride some of the most important long-distance north-south routes; the M1, A1 and the main-line railways from London to Edinburgh, Leeds, Sheffield and Nottingham daily carry thousands through a landscape that one suspects few will give a second glance. They might well recall an industrial scene, the towering chimneys of the brick works south of Bedford and Peterborough and the acrid smell of the brick firing that pervades the atmosphere for miles around. Or it might be the sight of intensive market-garden cultivation in eastern Bedfordshire, a scene which at the right time of year might also be recognised by a distinctive smell, that produced by countless acres of brussels sprouts!

With such reminders of the modern use of the landscape one could perhaps be forgiven for failing to recognise the features of a past age or in finding the topography anything but flat and uninteresting. The natural landscape of Bedfordshire and Huntingdonshire has no dramatic contrasts and views are often wide and unbroken by hill or deep valley. But this subtle landscape was an inspiration for one of England's great writers and preachers, John Bunyan, born at Elstow near Bedford. Bunyan's father was a travelling tinker and in his childhood John Bunyan must have spent much of his time in the lanes of central Bedfordshire. That countryside was to form the backcloth of *Pilgrim's Progress,* and although the scene has changed considerably over the last three hundred years much of Bunyan's inspiration can still be recognised. Not all of the locations are easily identified but few can disagree on the House Beautiful, where Pilgrim had sought shelter after his ascent of the Hill Difficulty, as the beautiful ruin of Houghton House perched on the top of a scarp to the north of Ampthill. Bunyan would almost certainly have known the footpath that runs north from the ruin, rather than the modern road that lies to the west. In his day the house was but newly built, one of the largest of the new country houses of early seventeenth-century Bedfordshire and unusual, even in a brick-making area, for its brick construction.

Pilgrim began his journey in the City of Destruction, the town of Bedford for which Bunyan can have had little sympathy as he is believed to have written part of the *Progress* while in a Bedford prison. Later he was to become minister of one of its non-conformist churches. Between the City and the Hill Difficulty lay the Slough of Despond. Some have sought to associate this with the Great North Road at Tempsford, where until the middle of the eighteenth century travellers had to cope with a ford over the River Ouse and a road which ran dangerously close to the river through a low marshy area that must have been a quagmire in the winter. But the clay vale that lies to the south of Bedford fits the description just as well. In Bunyan's day it was poorly drained and was used for pasture, with a few small brick kilns scattered among the fields; now the area is being eaten up by the huge pits of the London Brick Company. On a damp winter's day when a pall of smoke hangs over the fields, who can doubt how apt Bunyan's description still remains?

Although the natural landscape may lack visual excitement, it does reveal a high degree of variation produced by the range of geological strata across the two counties. Whilst thick layers of glacial boulder clay cover most of the bedrock the older solid geology can be recognised in building materials that range from soft chalk—clunch—through brick-clay to sandstone and oolitic limestone. In the south of Bedfordshire flints have also been used for domestic buildings and churches whereas elsewhere they have been relegated to farm outbuildings. The greatest variety in the use of materials can be seen in a short transect from the top of the Chalk scarp, between Dunstable and Luton, and the countryside just north of the River Ouse. In that short journey of fifteen miles the transition is made between a landscape that is clearly of an East Anglian appearance and one that is more familiar in the great stone-belt of the Cotswolds; from a mixed building style where construction is in flint, brick and timber to one where stone is universal and the style apparently ageless.

The geological strata run diagonally from south-west to north-east across Bedfordshire, swinging to a more northerly position through Huntingdonshire. The highest points lie in the extreme south on the top of the Chalk escarpment of the Chilterns, reaching to over 800 feet on the downs above Dunstable. From there a gradual fall in altitude continues north-eastwards until we reach the black peats of the Bedford Level at Ramsey St Mary in Huntingdonshire that lie below mean sea level. This slope is broken by two major river valleys, the Ouse and the Nene. The Nene forms the northern boundary of our area and marks the ancient limit of Huntingdonshire with the former Soke of Peterborough, while the Ouse has a long, meandering course through central Bedfordshire and southern Huntingdonshire before its entry into the Fens. With their tributaries, the Ivel, Kym, Hiz and Alconbury Brook the rivers have much to tell us of the early development of agriculture and settlement, their gravels rivalling the more traditional chalklands with their concentrations of prehistoric communities. Later the rivers served as a vital source of power to drive the many mills that were established across them. Domesday Book recorded sixty-three mills in Bedfordshire and another twenty-three locations in Huntingdonshire, nearly all of them water mills in parishes that lay astride or along one of the large rivers. Those riverside parishes had the most prosperous of the eleventh-century villages, and a glance at the 1:50,000 Ordnance Survey map will reveal how closely they were clustered. In the same way the steady growth of the small towns before the nineteenth century can be clearly related to the main rivers and the trade that they engendered.

Most of Huntingdonshire's solid geology is hidden by glacial drift although the oolitic limestone which underlies the western half of the county can be seen at the surface on the banks of the Nene where it forms the boundary with Northamptonshire. Small cuts in the bank indicate where the stone has been quarried in the past for local use and in the parish of Sibson-cum-Stibbington several larger quarries remain. Five hundred yards south of Stibbington House a small quay stands next to the abandoned stone quarry. Most of the rest of the county is characterised by a gently rolling countryside broken only occasionally by wide, shallow river valleys which are themselves partly filled with glacially derived material. North of the Huntingdon–Kettering road, the A604, lies an area of higher ground long noted for its heavy, poorly drained soils. Apart from the once unproductive Fens this has always been the most marginal of the county's agricultural areas, characterised today by tiny, shrinking villages and dotted with deserted settlements. The Huntingdonshire Fens were empty of permanent settlement for over twelve centuries following the abandonment of fields during the Roman period, for they were composed of the black peat that defied all the efforts of medieval reclamation. So intractable were some parts that they still lay under water in the middle of the last century. To many these peat lands offer no attraction; for the superficial eye this busy landscape is one of the dullest in Britain. But the story of the drainage attempts in the seventeenth and eighteenth centuries makes fascinating reading and a little historical research reveals Roman waterways, medieval retreats, mill and pumping station sites, together with a great complexity of fields whose boundaries may date from any number of efforts at reclamation. In some areas the creation of tiny blocks of land has been the result of enclosing an area of common land upon which many used to pasture their few animals; in others the farm names can suggest that the land was formerly under the water of one of the numerous, shallow meres. Frog Hall, on the site of the great Whittlesey Mere, could not be more appropriately named.

The countryside of northern Bedfordshire is little different from the undulating claylands of Huntingdonshire and the histories of their landscapes lie together. South of the Ouse, however, the landscape is one of scarps and wide clay vales. The most southerly of the scarps, the Upper Chalk, makes only a brief appearance with a dramatic steep slope between Luton and Dunstable. To the east it runs through north Hertfordshire but as a less significant feature. Several miles north or in front of the scarp lies the lower scarp that marks the edge of the more resistant Lower Chalk. From this area came the clunch stone, a material readily recognised in the churches of Totternhoe and Dunstable Priory. Quarrying of the chalk still continues but now it is used for cement. Along the scarp edge the evidence of earlier quarrying is still to be seen in small, grass-covered hollows; the minor road from Streatley to Sharpenhoe has several along its edge where it runs downhill on the west of Sharpenhoe Clappers. The car park at the picnic site on the Knolls at Totternhoe lies within another. It is not clear when the stone was first quarried, but the village of Chalgrave takes its name from a chalk pit so the activity probably goes back a thousand years or more. This narrow bench of the Lower Chalk has good

25

loamy soils which together with the quarries would account for the prosperity of the villages in the eleventh century. Certainly the vale of Gault Clay which lies to its north was much less attractive and settlements were smaller.

The Gault Clay is but a minor feature in Bedfordshire's topography and the land rises quickly again northwards to the third of the county's scarps, that of the Lower Greensand. Today this is the most wooded part of Bedfordshire with extensive plantations on private estates and in the hands of the Forestry Commission. The Greensand with its poor, light soils stretches across the county in a wide and continuous belt from Leighton Buzzard in the west to Northill and Old Warden in the east, where it is broken by the broad valley of the River Ivel before appearing again in the prominent hill of Sandy Warren. Warren names abound, although many of them are now covered in woodland and no longer display the open, heathland character of the pre-enclosure landscape. The rural history of the Greensand country is complex and reflects the marginal nature of the soil for permanent agriculture. When the resources of the land have come under pressure then the wastes have been cleared and new communities developed, but the area has also witnessed a reversal of the process and like the upland clays of north Huntingdonshire, farms now stand where villages once flourished and warren or wood replace former cultivated fields. In the eleventh century the Greensand still had considerable areas of primeval woodland although the county as a whole was less densely forested than neighbouring Hertfordshire or Buckinghamshire. An analysis of the swine figures for individual Domesday manors, the method by which woodland was estimated by the eleventh-century surveyors in Bedfordshire, suggests a fairly heavily timbered country between Woburn, Flitwick and Clophill.[1] Not surprisingly, this district has a complex pattern of villages and

[1] H. C. Darby and Campbell, E. M. J. (Eds.), *The Domesday Geography of South-East England* (1962), pp. 1-47.

hamlets with a multiplicity of minor roads connecting them.

Like the Chalk, the Lower Greensand has also been quarried for its stone, a rough but usable brown-green sandstone that can be seen in many of the churches and some of the cottages of the region although its use for domestic buildings appears to have been superseded by brick during the eighteenth century. Not a stone to be easily worked, it occurs most commonly in walls and church towers. The tower at Husborne Crawley has surely the greenest greensand to be seen anywhere for elsewhere a dull brown is predominant. But the use of this material pales into insignificance when compared with the value of the brick clays that lie at the foot of the Lower Greensand scarp. The series of deposits that comprise the Upper Jurassic Clays are not all suitable for brick manufacture, but those which lie to the south of Bedford and around Fletton in Huntingdonshire are eminently so. The name Fletton has become synonymous with a high-quality, hard-surface brick and the two areas provide up to half of the country's brick production. Not just in the local region close to the brick works but over the whole of southern and eastern England, brick from the huge clay pits has come to replace the former traditional materials of timber and plaster. Yet the best examples of early brick buildings are not to be found close to the brick kilns of today.

Despite the considerable variations to be encountered in the fertility of the soils of the scarp and vale country, south Bedfordshire has long been the more favoured region of the county. Few of the great landed proprietors held large estates in the northern claylands and it is significant that the documents held in the County Record Office are much richer from the southern parishes.

An understanding of the present natural landscape and the topography, its underlying geology, and the importance of the great rivers (Fig. 1) go some way towards an explanation of the development of the man-made landscape. But the

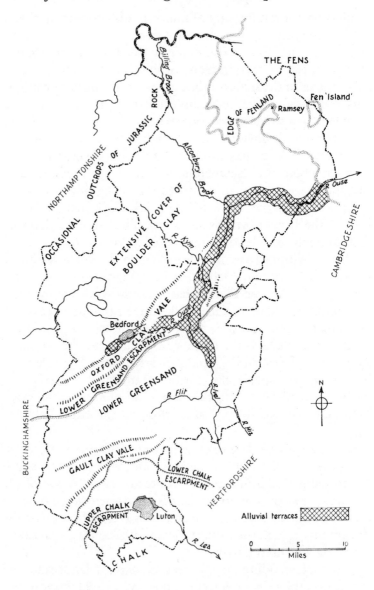

Fig. 1. The natural landscape.

landscape as we see it today presents only an inadequate impression of the conditions that man has faced in the past in the struggle to clear and cultivate a former wasteland. How much woodland had to be cleared before prehistoric farmers could cultivate their small, irregular fields and how far were the villages of the early Middle Ages still separated by acres of unused wasteland? These are the questions that need some consideration before we can go on to analyse the human landscape in detail. Maps and documents provide a full picture of the landscape over the past four hundred years, but most of the changes to the natural landscape appear to have taken place at an earlier date when the sources of data are far more fragmentary. Domesday Book throws some light on the former extent of woodland in eleventh-century Bedfordshire. For instance there was a huge wood at Luton. It was able to provide grazing for 2050 swine, and it lay to the south and east of the settlement, if place-names and the later history of the parish are to be believed as indicators of former woodland. Domesday Huntingdon-shire also had several tracts of relict woodland, the largest acreage occurring in Hurstingstone Hundred. This hundred was the most easterly of the county's four, with its farms and villages occupying the clayland to the south and west of the peat fen. It still contains most of the county's small area of deciduous woodland. Here the Domesday Book records woodland pasture in a different way from Bedford-shire, usually in terms of a measurement of so many leagues and occasionally in acres. The league was a common unit in medieval England, its 1500 paces roughly one and a half times the length of the modern mile. At Upwood there must therefore have been a considerable tract of woodland for it measured one and a half leagues long by one wide. And quite a number of the manors in Hurstingstone Hundred had woods that were a league square.

Apart from the woodland, Domesday Huntingdonshire reveals some evidence of large areas of waste or rough pasture within the Fens; though the references are not as frequent as one might expect from the many settlements that fringe the area. Only at Colne, Holywell and Warboys are substantial areas of marsh recorded and, together with a lengthy account of the fisheries of Whittlesey Mere and a fishery at Somersham, it might be surmised that much of the fen was indeed waste, too frequently flooded to be used even as common pasture.

Our knowledge of the natural landscape before the lengthy account of Domesday Book was compiled is very scanty. Documents are no longer available to describe the scene and we must fall back on an analysis of early place-names and the evidence that may be gleaned from the findings of archaeology. The two counties were well settled by the eleventh century and the majority of place-names recorded in Domesday Book are of Old English origin so we may be fairly sure that most of them date from the eighth century or earlier. Philologists recognise some place-name elements that provide clues to the character of the natural environment at the time when the settlements came into being. -Ley, -hurst, -wold and -field suggest areas still forested or but recently cleared. They occur quite frequently among the place-names of the two counties. Figure 2 shows those parishes where such place-name elements occur as well as a number of other places for which the woodland element is less immediately obvious, such as Grafham—the settlement by the grove— and Wootton—the tun or farm by the wood. Their distribution follows closely the pattern of woodland recorded several centuries later in Domesday Book. As those areas would certainly have witnessed a considerable amount of clearance throughout the Dark Ages we may see the Anglo-Saxons setting up their communities in a landscape that was still part of a forest environment. Conversely, those parts of the two counties where place-name and Domesday evidence make little mention of woodland were probably well cleared of forest before the arrival of the Anglo-Saxons. We cannot

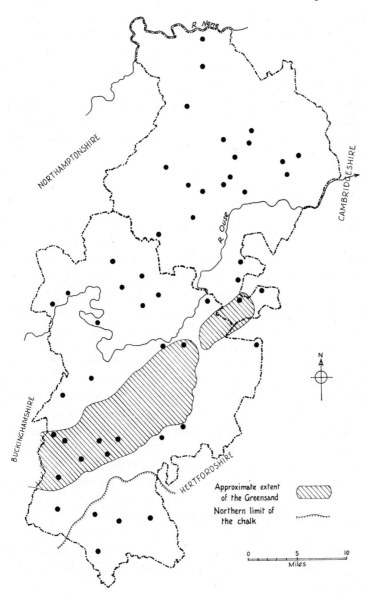

Fig. 2. The extent of Dark Age woodland revealed in place-names.

be sure how much woodland there was before man first began to settle the Ouse valley and the Chalk hills, but it is likely that the claylands and river terraces supported a mixed deciduous forest in which the oak was the dominant species, and the open chalkland would have been an area of woods and open glades. It is the activity of prehistoric man in clearing the forest, first for his animals to browse and then to provide a small area for cultivation, which we should turn to next.

Prehistoric settlers

The sites occupied by paleolithic man in Bedfordshire and Huntingdonshire are so few that it would be foolish to generalise about their distribution. A number of the Neolithic and Bronze Age locations have revealed the occasional flint that has been shaped in a much earlier age but they are not in themselves sufficient to recognise any form of settlement, no matter how temporary. Only in the peat fen does the number of finds give some justification for believing that the area was inhabited at least during the Mesolithic period. Here the finds occur beneath a layer of estuarine clay that was deposited between 1300 and 300 B.C., a time when the peat fen was flooded as the result of a marine transgression. At this time the fens were unsuitable for settlement and the Bronze and Iron Age communities of that period chose instead to dwell on the surrounding skirtland. Earlier still, some eight thousand years ago, when Mesolithic hunters roamed the area, the peat fen was a much drier place, much more habitable perhaps than in the Middle Ages. Even so, it is not unlikely that the economy of the Mesolithic hunters involved fishing in the rivers and meres. For instance, in the peat of Wistow Fen a small canoe has been found which may date from Mesolithic times.

The Mesolithic hunting communities must have made little impact upon the natural landscape, and there is certainly nothing in the present countryside that can be attributed to them. With the coming of Neolithic settlers and the first agricultural techniques during the fourth millennium B.C. the clearance of the primeval forest began and a change came over the landscape which was to have a permanent effect. There is no archaeological evidence from the Bedfordshire chalklands to substantiate this view but pollen analysis from sites elsewhere in the Chilterns and on the Chalk in East Anglia have noted a sharp decline in the quantity of tree seeds at the time that Neolithic settlements were being established. A corresponding increase in the quantity of weed seeds has suggested that some of the cleared land was being used for grazing and the climax vegetation was therefore unable to re-establish itself. Some of the land was cultivated and the excavation of a Bronze and Neolithic site at Barton Hill Farm, on the bench of the Lower Chalk on the outskirts of Luton, has revealed grain seeds that prove the presence of farming in the area around 1500 B.C.[2]

There is little visible evidence of the Neolithic period and the Early Bronze Age in the two counties. A number of earthen burial mounds or tumuli survive on the top of the scarp of the Upper Chalk, of which the most notable is the small cemetery group known as the Five Knolls overlooking the western suburbs of Dunstable. Others are known from archaeological records but have disappeared from the landscape as a result of ploughing. A more intriguing vestige of these early cultivators survives in the Chalk country in the form of ditched and banked enclosures. Along the outcrop of the Chalk runs the ancient prehistoric track known as the Icknield Way, a route that may still be traced for much of its length from Dorset to the north Norfolk coast. Through Bedfordshire it is overlain for greater part by minor roads, although the main road between Dunstable and Luton probably follows the line of the Icknield Way. Prehistoric re-

[2] Dyer, J. F., 'Neolithic and Bronze Age sites at Barton Hill Farm, Bedfordshire', *Bedfordshire Archaeological Journal,* 1 (1963), pp. 1–24.

mains, metal fragments, flints and pottery sherds have been reported as casual finds from many of the fields that border the Way, and most of the major sites lie a mile or two removed from this ancient route. Two exceptions are Waulud's Bank at Leagrave and the enclosure on the side of Galley Hill, both of them beside the Icknield Way and on the northern outskirts of Luton. Waulud's Bank is possibly one of the oldest and certainly one of the most puzzling of the prehistoric monuments in Bedfordshire. It survives as a low horse-shoe shaped bank around the headwaters of the River Lea, a small spring that emerges from the Chalk just north of the railway station at Leagrave, alongside the Icknield Way. Excavation has produced proof of occupation within the enclosure in the Neolithic period although the only evidence of building was a small hut, its floor scooped out from the ground. Then the site had been abandoned for over 1500 years until the late Iron Age when it was again occupied for a short period.[3] The age of the enclosure that lies on the side of Galley Hill is more difficult as excavation has so far failed to produce enough datable material, but the faint outline of ditch and rampart that can be seen in the field, although partly obscured by a golf course, may well belong to the Iron Age rather than earlier. However, the Iron Age ditches or Drays Ditches, as they are known, lie over and enclose an earlier ditched area. The purpose of such an enclosure remains a matter for conjecture and may well have changed when it was enlarged in the Iron Age. Was this a defensive work, guarding the prehistoric trackway, or was it used as some form of cattle corral when free-ranging animals were rounded up and checked? There is no evidence for settlement within its banks.

The third visible monument of the area lies just to the west of Dunstable at Maiden Bower, its banked enclosure

---

[3] Dyer, J. F. (1955) 'A Secondary Neolithic camp at Waulud's Bank, Leagrave, Bedfordshire', *The Bedfordshire Archaeologist,* 1, No. 1, and *The Bedfordshire Archaeological Journal* (1964), 2, pp. 1–15.

perched precariously on the edge of a chalk pit at the top of the Lower Chalk scarp. The Icknield Way lies a mile to the south (Plate 1). What can be seen on the surface is the defensive work of a small Iron Age camp but underneath lies a Neolithic causewayed camp, a circular series of ditches interrupted by 'causeways' that allowed access into the centre. Since the excavation of the now well-known example at Windmill Hill a number of these camps, as they are rather erroneously called, have been found and several have also been excavated. Dr Isobel Smith, in her report on the excavation at Windmill Hill, described them as a 'rallying point' for the population of a large area and some religious use has been attached to others from the discovery of pieces of human bone and infant burials in some of the ditches. Whatever their purpose, the existence of this communal centre at Maiden Bower, together with Waulud's Bank and the location of an Early Bronze Age 'henge' monument close to Barton Hill Farm, point to a fairly substantial population in the Chalk country in the Neolithic and Early Bronze Age. These peoples probably reached the area from the south-west, following the lighter soils that were to be found on the Chalk.

It would be wrong, however, to regard the Chalk as the sole centre of early prehistoric communities. Although most of the surface remains are found in that area the use of aerial photographs, particularly those produced by Dr J. K. St Joseph's Department of Aerial Photography at the University of Cambridge, has greatly expanded our knowledge of prehistoric and more recent landscape patterns that lie hidden just below the ploughed fields of the present day. Another causewayed camp has been located in Bedfordshire, but in mid-county at Cardington and some distance therefore from the traditional chalklands. The river gravels have come in to prominence and sites are now known along the whole length of the River Ouse. On the lower reaches the opening up of sand and gravel pits has brought to light much evidence of prehistoric settlement, although continuing excavation has also destroyed these freshly revealed artefacts of early man. At Little Paxton gravel working has produced evidence over quite an extensive area for Neolithic and Bronze Age settlement. The third region, that of the peat fen, has already been mentioned but there the earlier layers of human occupation are overlain by extensive remains of Iron Age field systems that produce a most complicated pattern when viewed from the air.

While these three tracts—the chalkland, the river gravels and peat fen—can now be recognised as the main locations of Neolithic and Bronze Age Man, the forested claylands can be seen to be not entirely empty. For instance, there are Beaker burials at Clifton and Brampton, both not far from important rivers. It is with the close of the Bronze Age, however, some two and a half thousand years ago that there is evidence of man's first persistent occupation and exploitation of the claylands and the Lower Greensand. At first it is likely that the newcomers, the pioneering colonists of the Iron Age, settled on the Chalk, following trackways long in use but this time approaching from the east and north-east. Bedfordshire has no major hill forts although the southern end of Sharpenhoe Clappers, with its extensive views northwards over the centre of the county, does have a bank that blocks the only easy route on to the promontory. Maiden Bower was of course fortified but this was almost certainly subsidiary to the large oval fort that is known as Ravensburgh Castle, lying just over the boundary in Hertfordshire. The county came under the sway of powerful Celtic warlords whose centre of power lay some miles to the south at Wheathampstead and St Albans, the latter the stronghold of the Belgic Catuvellauni tribe when the Romans made their second and permanent arrival in A.D. 43. North of the Chalk it is difficult to follow the influence of the Hertfordshire tribes although their coins have been found over much of Bedfordshire. On the Lower Greensand a small camp was constructed at Sandy—Caesar's Camp, in the grounds of The Lodge, now the headquarters of the Royal Society for the Protection of Birds.

One cannot deny that the prehistoric landscapes of Bedfordshire and Huntingdon, as we know them today, are lacking in the striking visual objects that have survived so well in other parts of Britain. The importance of the prehistoric centuries lie in the understanding they provide of the later patterns of field and farm, for it will be seen in the following chapters that those areas that were settled by the early farmers were to be chosen by the newcomers of the Roman and Saxon periods, providing a continuity in the rural scene that stretches back in some parts over four thousand years or more.

The Roman intrusion

The invasions of the Roman army can have meant little for many of the native communities of Bedfordshire and Huntingdonshire and for decades after the arrival of Roman rule life went on as usual with the new elements of an alien civilisation permeating only slowly into native society. But by the end of four centuries of Roman occupation the two counties were very much part of the civil zone that covered lowland Britain. New towns, roads and imperial estates were the main achievements of the occupiers, but native settlements had absorbed many elements of the Roman way of life using Roman methods of pottery and metal making. Even so, the two counties had been less 'romanised' than their neighbours to the south; here there are no large towns or opulent villas to boast of.

The present archaeological record of Romano-British sites reveals a fairly uniform spread of settlement across the two counties, which means that the claylands of north Bedfordshire and Huntingdonshire had attracted permanent occupation for the first time. But most of the settlements are small

37

and the absence of villas demonstrates the low value placed upon the claylands. The attractiveness of the river gravels and the borderland of the peat fen were such as to encourage a great expansion of fields and farming communities during the Roman period.

During the second century A.D. an official Roman interest was shown in the margins of the fenland, that mixture of clays and peat that runs along the peat fen proper, several miles in width and lying approximately at the twenty-five foot level. For at least two thousand years this had been a rich farming region, but now it came to be regarded as a provider of grain for the Roman legions stationed further north on the frontiers of Britain. This new exploitation came at a time when the fens were less water-logged and not as liable to flood; the siltlands at least could be opened up to farming. Aerial photographs show a great complex of fields, roadways and small hamlets running in a narrow corridor for mile after mile around the edge of the peat in north-east Huntingdonshire. Within the parishes of Colne and Somersham lie some of the most extensive field systems and until the plough-up campaign of the last war faint surface features could still be seen at Camp Ground, Colne, a field which lies close to Colnefield Farm on the edge of the higher ground. Here was a small Romano-British settlement. Nearby were two groups of parallel ditches leading down to the peat which have been interpreted as docks or slipways, lending support to the idea that this area was part of a huge imperial estate that exported grain through the fenland river system.

Yet if the ancient field systems of Colne belonged to a Roman estate, it must be recognised that the site has failed to reveal any substantial buildings that would have been a necessary part of such an economic organisation. A structure built of Barnack stone stood close to another settlement complex at Knobb's Farm, in the neighbouring parish of Somersham. Sylvia Hallam believes that the two parishes stand for a villa-village relationship, a pattern that archaeologists have come to recognise over much of lowland England in recent years. Similar associations have been found by Dr Hallam in other villages on the edge of the fens at Hockwold, Brandon, Denver and Stonea.[4]

Aerial photographs support the archaeological evidence that the peat fen in this district of Huntingdonshire remained unsuitable for cultivation and they show its eastern edge lying along the Coln Ditch. The survival of the British name is significant here for philologists agree that the village of Colne has taken its name from the water course. The Ditch forms part of a long system of waterways, known as the Car Dyke, that skirt around the fen. This canal, for such it was over much of its length, was constructed in the Roman period to transport grain, leather and wool from the fertile lands of the fenland fringe northwards to Lincoln and the frontier settlements on Hadrian's Wall. The Coln Ditch is said to follow the old western course of the River Ouse, but what survives in the landscape today is certainly an artificial cut. Its sinuous character is best seen at the southern end where the Ditch meets the much straighter and more recent Old Bedford River. That this is a man-made feature of the landscape is suggested by the high bank on its eastern side, the direction from which flooding would be expected. The absence of silt in the deep black, peat soil that lies on either side argues against the view that the Coln Ditch is the old abandoned water course of a major river. South of the Old and New Bedford Rivers the course can only be traced with difficulty to a junction with the present line of the Ouse east of Earith. On following the Ouse downstream for several miles it is again evident on the right bank, but this time in Cambridgeshire, with an artificial cut running southwards to a junction with the River Cam at Waterbeach. Christopher Taylor has already described the use of the Car

[4] Hallam, S., 'The settlement around the Fens' in C. W. Phillips (Ed.), *The Fenland in Roman Times,* Royal Geographical Society Research Series, no. 5 (1970), pp. 22–113.

Dyke and other artificial cuts in Roman Cambridgeshire[5] for transporting produce northwards and we can imagine those barges passing through the fenland rivers and canals, eventually along the Coln Ditch where the produce would have been augmented from the fields of Somersham and Colne.

Northwards the route of the Car Dyke is not very easy to trace although it does re-emerge in places. At Park Farm, Ramsey, the line of a banked ditch can still be seen that bears little relationship to the present drainage of the area. The Car Dyke must have made a diversion around the 'island' of Ramsey, an isolated site first occupied in the tenth century A.D. by a group of monks; it can be recognised again to the north of the town, close to Bodsey House. North from the house runs a minor road, through Ramsey Mereside to Pondersbridge; it is followed by the Roman waterway, although here it has acquired the erroneous name of Cnut's Dyke. Finally in Farcet Fen, north of Pondersbridge, the twisting line of the Oakley Ditch, which forms the boundary between the old counties of Huntingdonshire and Cambridgeshire, takes the canal out of the county across the Nene. The antiquity of the Oakley Ditch is unmistakable for it acts as a boundary for a great number of otherwise regular shaped fields that were laid out when this part of the great marsh was drained in the seventeenth and eighteenth centuries, utilising one boundary that was already fixed.

Like the fenland edge, the river gravels had long been settled by the time of the Roman incursion. Yet here again there was a noticeable increase in activity and an expansion of the cultivated area. Aerial photographs have provided a much fuller picture than either the landscape itself—where scarcely any visible traces survive—or archaeological finds have indicated. On the upper reaches of the Ouse, for example, the parishes of Harrold and Odell have revealed a most intricate pattern of, largely, Romano-British fields. There is nothing to be seen on the surface now. Again

[5] Taylor, C. C., *The Cambridgeshire Landscape* (1973), p. 41.

between Cople and Willington, downstream from Bedford, another system of fields together with roads, field lanes and buildings can be seen from the air. A third important area was on the gravels of the River Ivel, centred on the parishes of Northill, Southill, Sandy and Biggleswade.

The level terrace on the west bank of the Ivel is rich with the evidence of Romano-British fields. The pre-Roman occupation of the area is suggested by a small native settlement at Sandy and the univallate late Iron Age fort of Caesar's Camp that stands less than a mile to the south. On Quince Hill, Old Warden, another peculiar earthwork may be of a similar date. A small Roman town developed at Sandy. It was discovered in the middle of the last century with the building of the railway. Roman Sandy was never anything more than a local centre, probably succeeding the native settlement to the west when a number of Roman roads were constructed. Between Biggleswade and Sandy the main road cannot be followed on the ground although it has left traces in the place-name of Stretton or Stratton, a former hamlet to the south of Biggleswade, and Stratford, where the road crossed a brook into Sandy. It is interesting to note that although the Roman town remained undiscovered until just over a hundred years ago the field in which it lay had long been known as Chester Field.

On the opposite side of the River Ouse in Northill parish, close to the hamlet of Upper Caldecote, part of a rectangular grid of fields has been observed. The fields must have been very small, with ditches or field roads surrounding them, and they were contained within a larger square enclosure. Their regularity and their strict adherence of long-axis orientation to a line that is very slightly west of a due south-north direction strongly suggests that here is a survival of a Roman organised field system, commonly known as centuriation. But the crop marks of the aerial photographs are even more interesting when compared with features of the present landscape, a landscape that still seems to bear the marks of the Roman surveyors. Roads and farm tracks, bridleways and footpaths still enclose the fields in a grid-like form. Yet this was not an area where the topography was reshaped by an act of parliamentary enclosure in the eighteenth century. In fact earlier maps show that the pattern of communications is not a recent one. What is more significant is that one of the boundary roads of the Roman square can be seen to join on to an existing road. A minor Roman road runs westward across the area from the northern edge of Biggleswade towards Quince Hill. Hill Lane, as it is now known, almost certainly ran up to a small defensive work or lookout. And it is significant that the parish in which it lies, Old Warden, takes its Old English name from such a feature, which must still have been prominent when the Anglo-Saxons settled the area. A thousand yards north of the Hill Lane, and parallel to it, lies another minor roadway that runs westwards from Ivel Farm through Upper Caldecote to Ickwell Green. Northwards again and at a distance of just over seven hundred yards, a long footpath forms a third parallel line. Dividing this system into blocks of fields are a number of roads and tracks running roughly north-south and a regular distance apart (Fig. 3). This planning of land and communications is a remarkable survival from the Roman period into the twentieth century. Better examples are known elsewhere in Lowland England, where the grid system confirms rather more readily to the normal Roman measurements of twenty actus square, or 776 yards square, but the evidence here is clear, backed as it is by the crop marks that are visible from the air (see Plate 2). There will be occasion to return to this fascinating and ancient fragment of the Bedfordshire landscape in the next chapter.

By the second century A.D. a major new area of settlement was emerging in northern Huntingdonshire, centred on the new Roman town of Durobrivae. The faint outline of the outer ramparts of the town can still be seen alongside the A1 road in the north of Chesterton parish—where the place-

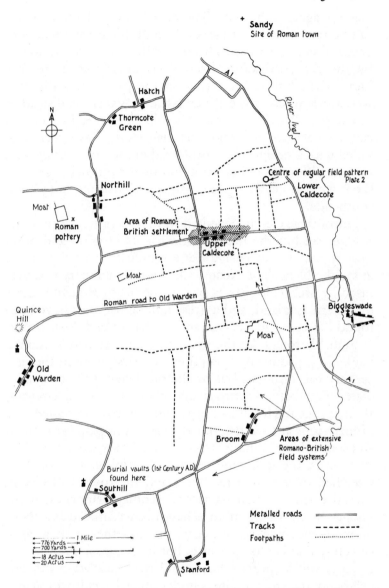

Fig. 3. Early roads and fields, Northill and Southill. The landscape of regular roads and paths conforms well to Roman measures of a centuriation pattern.

name is again important. The raised line of Ermine Street can be recognised as it passes through the former southern gate and in to the town. This major Roman road is followed by the A1 northwards from Alconbury until it reaches Durobrivae but at some time in the past it was diverted westwards to cross the River Nene at Wansford instead of crossing at Water Newton. The old bridgehead—and it is certain that such an important road would have been provided with a bridge—was protected in the first century A.D. by a small fort on either bank, but by the following century the town had grown up and had superseded the fort on the south side.

Durobrivae clearly benefited from its location close to the bridgehead but the main reason for its creation and rapid growth was the extensive pottery industry that developed along the Nene. The Nene Valley pottery industry is recognised by archaeologists as one of the major Roman centres of eastern England, and a great number of kilns have been found between Durobrivae and Wansford and downstream around Fletton. Like the town the industry had a humble beginning, producing quantities of coarse ware in the first century for local use, but by the third century finer quality wares were being sent to many other parts of the country. By that time the town had begun to outgrow its walled area of forty-four acres and suburbs were developing both north and south along Ermine Street. When the settlement reached its peak in the following century the ribbon development stretched over a hundred acres and the town had clearly exceeded the size that its second century planners had envisaged. Some of the suburbs have been examined as a result of road widening some years ago, together with a large cemetery that lay to the south, but it remains a pity that the town is still in private hands and that excavation has not been undertaken. The site is under intensive cultivation and the ploughing that is carried out every year must be damaging the remains of streets and buildings. Aerial photographs have recorded the street pattern, however, and that is rather remarkable for the way in which it lies askew to Ermine Street—a feature for which no clear explanation has been produced. Could it be that the proto-town lay alongside the road but that when it became more successful it was decided to divert the road so that it passed through the settlement? Only a full excavation can unravel the topographical history of this important Roman town.

In spite of the lack of systematic excavation two very important finds have been made from within the walls of Durobrivae by field researchers. In 1974 a hoard of valuable gold coins was found, most of them datable to circa A.D. 350. Then in the following year came a find that may well rival the well-known Mildenhall Treasure in its significance. A hoard of silver vessels of the third and fourth centuries was found to contain a number of pieces that may have belonged to a Christian community—a goblet, probably used as a chalice, a hanging bowl with a Christian inscription, and a long handled strainer that might have been used as a filter for communion wine. This set of communion vessels had been hidden, buried to escape detection and it is fascinating to speculate whether the owners feared persecution from heathen invaders, the Anglo-Saxons, or from amongst their fellows. Such finds are an indication not just of a Christian community in a Roman town, but they reflect too the wealth that the town had created, a wealth and influence which has led John Wacher to believe that we should attribute cantonal capital status to Durobrivae.[6] Several villas in the country-side about the town certainly suggest that it had become the centre of a prosperous agricultural and industrial landscape. The villas that are found clustered around the towns of Roman Britain were as dependent upon those towns, as the markets for their produce, as those towns were upon the produce of the villa estates. Godmanchester was the only other town in Roman Bedfordshire and Huntingdonshire.

[6] *Current Archaeology*, No. 54 (1976), pp. 199–204.

Godmund's caester or fort was the name given by the Anglo-Saxons to the ruins that they encountered there. We do not know its Roman name. The town developed in a similar way to Durobrivae, for it was built on an important road, this time the junction of the Via Devana—on its route from Cambridge to Leicester—and Ermine Street, where a crossing was made of the River Ouse. By the close of the second century a wall had replaced an earlier ditch, enclosing a town of twenty acres. Although the walls have long since disappeared, the line that they took can be followed along the streets that form a polygonal centre to the little town— the Causeway, Old Court Hall, London Street, Earning Street and Cambridge (formerly East) Street. Excavations have located the position of the south gate, which stood with two gate-towers flanking the thirty-foot wide Ermine Street, the road spanned by a single arch. A town such as this, on an important road, would have been expected to provide accommodation for officials as they travelled the country on business. During the 1960s a series of baths and a *mansio,* or official guest house, were uncovered near Pinfold Lane, the second-century buildings having been built after a group of poorer huts had been cleared from the site. The *mansio* itself was destroyed by fire a hundred years or so after its construction and was not replaced.[7] To the north of the town and close to the now abandoned railway line from Huntingdon to St Ives a small corridor villa has been discovered. In use from the second to the fourth century it was almost certainly connected with Godmanchester. Close to the house stood a large timber structure which might have been a barn but which the excavator, W. H. Frend, considered to have served as a dwelling for the labourers employed on the villa-estate.[8]

[7] A report on the 1968 excavations at Pinfold Lane, Godmanchester, is contained in the *Proceedings of the Cambridge Antiquarian Soc.,* XLI (1968).

[8] Frend, W. H., 'A Roman farm settlement at Godmanchester', *Proc. Camb. Ant. Soc.,* XLI (1968).

In the prosperous days of the second and third century urban life flourished in Roman Britain. At Durobrivae extensive suburbs had developed and the same was to occur at Godmanchester. But the non-replacement of the *mansio* might signify that the town was already losing some of its importance and prosperity. By the end of the fourth century there is evidence of a squatter settlement in the villa and we may suspect that town life was also decaying.

These three areas of settlement dominated the landscape of Roman Bedfordshire and Huntingdonshire, their prosperity was partly the result of good agricultural resources and partly an outcome of industrial exploitation. We now know that the farmers of the Roman period were capable of exploiting the heavier claylands, equipped with a new plough that had an iron coulter blade and a share that cut deeper and was stronger than its prehistoric counterpart. Yet the evidence from the two counties is not of a large-scale movement on to the wooded claylands. Settlement sites are known and their numbers continue to increase but there is little evidence, as yet, to suggest that any of the colonisation was the result of Roman influence and interest. The Romans did, however, construct their roads throughout the whole of the two counties (Fig. 4).

The main roads, Watling Street and Ermine Street, are both well known and are followed for most of their length by the modern roads of the A5 and A1. Much less certainty exists about the minor Roman roads and their alignments are hard to find from Ordnance Survey maps although the work of the Viatores, as elsewhere in eastern England, has done much to clarify and fill in the gaps. A good example of the confusion that can arise comes from the road that ran between the Roman settlements of Sandy and Godmanchester. Four miles north of Sandy, just east of Highfield Farm, a long, straight route runs for nine miles to Godmanchester, in part a green lane but in others nothing more than a footpath. The Ordnance Survey 1:25,000 First Series

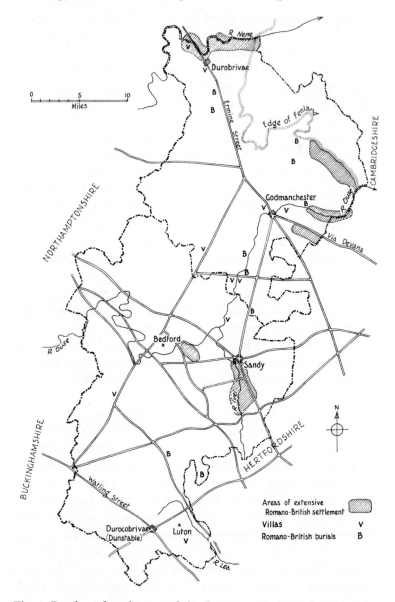

Fig. 4. Roads and settlement of the Roman period (roads after the Viatores).

map, commonly known as the 2½″, marks the track as 'Roman Way' on that part of its route through Toseland and St Neots Rural. But recent aerial photographs have located another road, running dead straight and lying a mile or so to the west. This is the Roman road that the Ordnance Survey now mark on their 1″ and 1:50,000 maps. A mystery now envelops the original Roman Way. Was it an alternative route that was little used in Roman times but rose to prominence later? Its avoidance of any settlement, apart from Toseland, is unusual for a route of such a length. Toseland was the centre of one of the Saxon Hundreds, so was the so-called Roman Way perhaps a Dark Age trackway along which the men of the Hundred travelled to their meeting place?

Many Roman roads have disappeared and can only be found by aerial reconnaissance or the chance digging up of road metal. In other cases they are followed by minor roads, although these are not easy to identify in the two counties, and the overall impression is that the close of the Roman period saw the abandonment of many routes. In one or two places, however, the raised agger or curved surface of the Roman road can still be seen in the landscape. One of the best examples is in Claypits Field, Old Warden (Plate 3). A fine raised track, ditched on either side and some thirty feet in width, runs northwards to Warden Street. The Viatores have traced the line of a road from Shefford to a crossing of the Ouse a few miles downstream from Bedford. At least, it is assumed the road crossed the river although there is no evidence on the north bank and no settlement that it could have served—but a thirty-foot road was no small road for the Romans to build. The Bedfordshire volume of the English Place-Name Society is not helpful either about the derivation of the name Warden Street, describing it as one of the few that do not appear to refer to a Roman road. But the evidence from Claypits Field cannot be denied and the discovery of the important Romano-British settlement area with its network of fields and lanes between Willington and Cople now provides a more logical reason for the route of the road as it points in this direction.

Another piece of Roman road probably survives at Elton in northern Huntingdonshire although only excavation can make the matter certain. East of Over End and to the south of the minor road that runs to Haddon a pasture contains the relic feature of ridge-and-furrow, the long, narrow strips of former arable that would have been a common sight in the medieval landscape. At right angles to the ridges is a substantial bank, running north-eastwards. In most cases such a feature would be recognised as the headland of the former open field, the piece of ground at either end of the field on which the plough-team would have been turned and that was ploughed last of all. But this bank breaks up two groups of ridges that are both running in the same direction and it is continued north of the road in the hedge-bank between two more fields. Its alignment also accords well with a known Roman road from Irchester in Northampton-shire to the crossing of the Nene at Water Newton. Just a few hundred yards north of Over End the alignment can be picked up on the north side of the A605 road, following minor road and footpath to the village at Water Newton.

The Roman roads gave rise to a number of new towns in Bedfordshire and Huntingdonshire, but with the gradual decay of Roman civilisation in Britain during the fourth century both roads and towns slowly fell into disuse. It was not just the larger centres that were affected, but much of the countryside must have gone on with the only way of life that they knew, farming, unaffected by the great political, social and cultural changes that were to be a part of the Roman withdrawal. Where a settlement depended heavily upon the traffic that passed upon the great roads, however, its decline must have been quite dramatic. Such was prob-ably the fate of Roman Dunstable, known as Durocobrivae. We know surprisingly little about this settlement but it must have developed astride the important routes of Watling Street and the Icknield Way. Present evidence points to a total collapse of the community, and the site returned to a cross-roads in the waste for more than seven hundred years before a new medieval town was raised over the same site.

The achievements of the Roman period had been considerable. For the first time the two counties were populated over most of their area, although the claylands and the Lower Greensand were but thinly peopled in comparison with the river gravels and the fenland edge. The Chalk no longer played the prominent role that had been its lot in prehistory. Apart from the great expansion of the rural areas, new towns and roads had been laid down and although much has failed to survive as visible features of the twentieth-century landscape we cannot understand the evolution of today's topography without a knowledge of the Roman past. It was into this settled scene that the first Anglo-Saxons began to establish their farms and to till the soil alongside their Romano-British neighbours, for there is no evidence of an emptying of the countryside in advance of the Germanic tribes and plenty of evidence that the land had room for both cultural groups to live at peace with one another. The 'takeover', when it came, was probably a peaceful affair and has enabled us to discern in the present landscape something of its Celtic past.

SELECT BIBLIOGRAPHY

Darby, H. C., 'Domesday woodland in Huntingdonshire', *Transactions of the Cambridgeshire and Huntingdonshire Archaeological Society*, V (1937).

Edmonds, E. A. and Dinham, C. H., *Geology of the Country around Huntingdon and Biggleswade* (1965).

Hardin, D. W., *The Iron Age in Lowland Britain* (1974).

Phillips, C. W. (Ed.), *The Fenland in Roman Times*, Royal Geographical Society Research Series, no. 5 (1970).

Taylor, C. C., *Fields in the English Landscape* (1975).
The Viatores, *Roman Roads in the South East Midlands* (1964).
Wacher, J., *The Towns of Roman Britain* (1975).

The volumes of the following journals contain numerous interesting reports of past or current archaeological sites within the two counties: *Bedfordshire Archaeologist; Bedfordshire Archaeological Journal; Journal of the Manshead Society; Proceedings of the Cambridgeshire Antiquarian Society.*

2. The English settlement

Change or continuity? Early boundaries. A Christian country.

Change or continuity?

SOME TWENTY YEARS ago the information that was available from archaeological sources concerning the nature of the Anglo-Saxon settlement following the Roman withdrawal was still very scanty and disconnected. Few writers would have disagreed with the contemporary and near-contemporary accounts of Gildas and Bede, that the fifth century was a time of turmoil and bloodshed, an invasion of Germanic hordes that was to obliterate all traces of the earlier Celtic patterns. But the wealth of evidence that has since become available has strongly challenged such a view and over most parts of Lowland Britain archaeologists are finding traces of a survival of the native British in what had become an English landscape. Historians and geographers have added their voices to the debate, each finding some facet of the earlier culture reflected in later patterns or as a clear survival in the post-Roman period whether it be in the form of place-names, field systems or an administrative structure. Yet there can be no denying that the English conquest did bring about change in the landscape, in some cases a dramatic change with the steady influx of new settlers.

It is currently fashionable to question a number of the previously held ideas drawn from research into Anglo-Saxon or Old English place-names. A critical reassessment of place-names and their meaning in the history of settlement is now going on. Some of the earlier volumes of the English Place-Name Society need to be read in the light of these new ideas.

The contents of the earlier volumes, including that for Bedfordshire and Huntingdonshire, need to be greatly expanded to include many more of the minor settlement and topographic names. But the new ideas in the realm of place-names do not contradict the fact that the two counties remain solidly English when the names of villages, hamlets and towns are plotted out from the map. A few settlements may be renamed Celtic places but we have no positive evidence in our area that this was a process of any importance. Others may have changed their name from an earlier English one, as we know happened in the case of St Ives, formerly called Slepe, but such known examples are of changes made several centuries after the Anglo-Saxon settlement.

Two place-name elements have commonly been recognised as indicative of the first phase of Anglo-Saxon colonisation— -ing (from -inga, -ingas) and -ham. Recently the 'ing' names have been challenged as the earliest of the English place-name elements,[1] but from its explanation of 'the people of', signifying perhaps a roaming tribal or kinship group, it may still be considered among the early place-name elements current in the fifth and sixth centuries. In Bedfordshire and Huntingdonshire *-ham* and *-ing* names are few in number, but they show some relationship with the main river valleys and the fertile loams. There is a corresponding avoidance of marshy areas and places where soils were thin or infertile. In other words, there is a strong preference for those same areas that had already been farmed for over two thousand years and which had become well peopled by Romano-British farmers. One particular group of Anglo-Saxon settlers can be recognised on the upper reaches of the Ouse, above Bedford, where early *-ham* elements occur in Biddenham, Bromham and Pavenham.

[1] Dodgson, J. M., 'The significance of the distribution of the English place-names in "ingas", "inga" in South-East England', *Medieval Archaeology*, 10, pp. 1–30 (1966).

The evidence of place-names can only give a crude impression of where the first English settlers established themselves, for such a method lacks precision both in time and location. With the latter we cannot be certain that the present settlement is in the same place as when it was first recorded in Domesday Book. Again, one cannot be sure that the Domesday site or the present village lie over the original Anglo-Saxon settlement. Indeed, recent work by archaeologists has shown that the stability of the English village is something of a myth and that it was not unusual for several sites to be tried out during the Dark Ages before a final choice was made. Sites at Little Paxton and Eaton Socon, for example, have revealed that the Late Saxon villages lay to one side of the present settlements and it cannot be long before other cases of the 'Mid-Saxon Shuffle' are found in the two counties.

It is unfortunate that archaeological evidence of the first Anglo-Saxons often reveals much about their burial customs but all too little about their day-to-day life. Early Saxon settlements are coming to light in southern and eastern England but none have so far been discovered in Bedfordshire or Huntingdonshire. However, the early burial grounds can still suggest much about the nature of the first settlements. Cremation urns of the fifth century have been found at Somersham and Luton. In the debris of an abandoned villa at Totternhoe fragments of pottery from the same period have revealed a squatter settlement. More important finds have come from Kempston, now a suburb of Bedford, and Sandy. At Kempston a large pagan cemetery, spanning over several generations, has produced a number of pots and urns that find their parallel in those uncovered from the camps of mercenary Saxon soldiers outside the gates of Roman York and Cambridge. Some of the fifth-century urns from Sandy were found as long ago as the middle of the eighteenth century and were labelled 'British' until recent reassessment identified them as belonging to a particular group of very early Anglo-Saxon urns known as the *Buckel-urnen*. These irregular shaped pots indicate a very early settlement at Sandy and their location within the area of the Roman town accords well with the idea that the first settlers were attracted to those parts that were being cultivated by the Romano-British. The Romano-British material found in association with the urns is insufficient to recognise an actual overlap in time of the two cultures.[2]

These finds of early fifth century pottery can only indicate to us that the Anglo-Saxons chose areas favoured by the Romano-British areas in which to settle. They cannot be used to prove or disprove continuity in a more specific way. But for several places the evidence from archaeological and other sources does point strongly to an overlap in time and location that is still partly reflected in the landscape. Northill has already been mentioned in the previous chapter as one example, where the landscape retains part of an organised or planned field system of the Roman period. The evidence there for a direct overlap of settlement patterns is perhaps just as clear. The names of Northill and Southill are themselves significant for they refer to the territory of the Gifle, a British tribe whose name is further recalled in the Ivel river, a British name, that forms the eastern boundary of the two parishes. Presumably their settlements were named by the Anglo-Saxons as lying north and south of the old watchtower (Old Warden, the parish that still divides them). At Northill substantial quantities of Roman pottery have been found in the woods to the west of the village and widely scattered around the hamlet of Upper Caldecote. The latter was first recorded in 1197 but its Old English name points to a settlement of much greater antiquity. The way the hamlet has developed along one of the east-west roads that formed part of the Roman centuriation system also suggests an English takeover of a Romano-British settlement. North-

[2] Kennet, D. H., 'The Anglo-Saxon cemetery at Sandy, Bedfordshire', *Medieval Archaeology*, XIV (1970), pp. 17–53.

ill and Southill both contain a number of hamlets, some of them mentioned in Domesday Book, and the location of Romano-British sites in the district shows a good relationship with them. In Southill two burial vaults of the first century A.D. have been found together with considerable quantities of Roman pottery.

The picture of this early settlement that emerges from the pages of Domesday Book suggests a well-cultivated landscape in the eleventh century. Old Warden had an estate of nine hides (approximately 1080 acres), a large area for any of the Bedfordshire manors and of even greater significance when it is realised that the western half of the parish lies on the infertile soils of the Lower Greensand. Southill's hamlets, Broom and Stanford, lying on river gravels, receive separate mention in Domesday Book. Broom had no less than five hides of arable land, even though no manorial demesne was mentioned. In Northill the manor comprised another six and a half hides and a further three hides were recorded in the possession of one Eudo, son of Hubert. Later details reveal that Eudo's three hides were in Ickwell and Upper Caldecote. Apart from its hamlets Southill also had over seven hides of land together with an extra-parochial hamlet at Shefford Hardwick. All the evidence of Domesday Book suggest a landscape fully cultivated by the eleventh century, a reflection of its importance to both Romano-British and Anglo-Saxon farmers, and one suspects that further archaeological finds will support the idea that the settlement pattern of this area is as much Celtic as it is Germanic in origin.

That the hamlets did not contain any land that was under the direct control of the manorial lord, as part of his own farm or demesne, is important. In other parts of England Professor Glanville Jones has recognised such Domesday hamlets as probable remnants of a former Celtic pattern of settlement, forming part of a large administrative unit known as a multiple estate. Professor Jones believes that such units survived in part the Anglo-Saxon 'invasions' and underlie English patterns of rural settlement.[3] The peculiar organisation of the English 'Soke' may be one way in which they can be recognised. The right to hold soke, or jurisdiction over, a group of settlements usually meant that they lay outside the control of the Hundred court, such courts dealing with a wide range of civil and criminal offences. The right was normally attached to one manor rather than to an individual, that manor therefore exercising control over a number of hamlets and villages in a much wider sense than the manor court. Somersham, for example, held the right of soke over the settlements of Colne, Bluntisham, Earith, Pidley and Fenton, a right that was still being exercised in the eighteenth century. These places shared a huge area of common grazing that lay on the higher ground between them, enclosed by the cultivated land of the settlements that lie in a semicircle around the edge of the Huntingdonshire peat fen and on the banks of the River Ouse. Each of the parishes has produced abundant evidence of intensive cultivation and settlement during the Roman period. Is the pattern here therefore of Celtic origin? There is some evidence for a Celtic survival in the dedication of Colne's church to St Helen, a fourth-century saint who is likely to have been known to Christians of the Roman period. Dedications to St Helen are rare, but the name appears again at Wheathampstead in Hertfordshire where the former Iron Age oppidum was succeeded by the present village.

The soke is even clearer at Eaton Socon where the term has become part of the place-name. Until its recent inclusion in Huntingdonshire separated Eaton Socon from its many hamlets this was the largest of the Bedfordshire parishes, covering over 7,600 acres. Of the hamlets of Bushmead, Staploe, Duloe, Upper Stondon, Honeydon, Begwary,

---

[3] See, for example; Jones, G. R. J., 'Settlement patterns in Anglo-Saxon England', *Antiquity*, 35 (1961), pp. 221–32, and 'Multiple Estates and Early Settlement' in Sawyer, P., *Medieval Settlement* (1976).

Colesden, Chawston and Wyboston only the last named was mentioned in Domesday Book. Yet the great size of Domesday Eaton, at twenty hides, shows that a number of the hamlets must be of pre-Domesday origin even if their details have been included with those of the parent manor. Some may be recognised from other evidence. Beggary or Begwary, for example, formed the core of land owned by the monks of St Neots Priory; it did not achieve manorial status until the thirteenth century. At Chawston there is archaeological evidence for the age of the hamlet where a homestead moat has yielded examples of Saxo-Norman pottery. The evidence for the Roman occupation of Eaton Socon is not as clear as it is for Northill-Southill but it is significant that a villa and settlement have been found close to the later medieval manor. Aerial photographs have located a large courtyard villa some several hundred yards north of the parish church.

A few yards across the River Ouse to the east of Eaton lay the former large parish of Eynesbury. A parish still survives, but today it is a small part only of a much larger unit. Pieces have been taken off to found the medieval town of St Neots and other parts were administered by a St Neots rural parish council. A third part became a separate parish of Eynesbury Hardwick. At Domesday Eynesbury held the soke over those areas, which included a number of hamlets —Cotes (probably Caldecote), Weald and Wintringham. Two large manors existed, one of them of nine hides and held formerly by Edward the Confessor. The other was even larger, at fifteen hides. Between them they were said to have fifty-five ploughs which would have been a massive total for just Eynesbury and must therefore reveal a large population established elsewhere in the parish—of which the embryonic town of St Neots would have been one. The archaeological evidence again proves to be instructive. Due east of the villa at Eaton Socon, but on the other side of the river, buildings of the third and fourth century A.D. have been found, close

to the present village of Eynesbury. Pottery, tiles and tes-
serae all suggest another villa site. The hamlets of Wintringham, Weald and Caldecote all lie close to the Roman road
that ran from Godmanchester to Sandy and coins, burials
and pottery of the Roman period have all been found in the
parish. Close to the medieval site of Monks Hardwick, where
the monks of St Neots had a grange, an indistinct set of
earthworks seen from the air have been attributed to a possible Roman camp and tumuli but the site has not been
excavated and there is nothing to see on the ground today.

Whatever the meaning of these ancient features of the
landscape—whether they are remnants of large villa estate
systems or were indeed part of a Celtic multiple estate—
there can be no mistaking that some form of continuity has
occurred between the Roman and Saxon periods in the most
favourable areas of Bedfordshire and Huntingdonshire. Yet
continuity, no matter how it is viewed, cannot provide a
satisfactory explanation for the location of the majority of
the villages and we must still recognise the great contribution made to the settlement landscape by the Anglo-Saxons,
although it is likely that their role as pioneers is going to be
reduced even further through new archaeological discoveries. They gave a new impetus to the colonisation of the
waste, just as the Romans had done, but their contribution
must be seen as part of a continuum of change that was to
go on adding to the landscape of settlement until well into
the Middle Ages.

By the eleventh century the map of villages was almost
complete over the two counties and even where Domesday
Book fails to record names their existence can be shown from
other contemporary sources. In Huntingdonshire, for example, the Inquisitio Eliensis and earlier documents help to
fill in the blanks of Domesday Book. In this way Stow
(Longa), Barham, Ramsey and Raveley can be located. The
south-west of Bedfordshire appears an empty quarter until
it is realised that the missing settlements of Heath and Reach,

Eggington, Stanbridge and Billington were all hamlets of the royal manor of Leighton, a manor that had been increased by ten hides after 1066 and had almost certainly absorbed some of them. That leaves but a few places on the modern map that were not mentioned by 1066. The most notable gaps are in Bedfordshire around Luton and on the clays north of Bedford, and in Huntingdonshire chiefly in the wooded Hurstingstone Hundred (where the hundred-name means 'the people of the wood'). There is little evidence for much Danish settlement although the Danes held sway over the whole of the area during the ninth century. Carlton and Toft are the only two Scandinavian place-names in Bedfordshire and there are only six for Huntingdonshire. Two of those, however, have also given their name to Hundreds, Toseland and Norman Cross. It seems likely that the number of Danish settlers was fairly small, but nevertheless one must remember that the stability of the Old English place-names may present a rather biased picture.

Several of the villages of the two counties have the same name as their neighbour or one that lies but a short distance away, differentiated only by additions such as Great or Little or the name of the manorial family of the early part of the Middle Ages—such as Offord Cluny and Offord Darcy. Cluny belonged to the Abbey of Cluny in France. The majority of these 'joint' parishes were undivided in the eleventh century although it would not always be wise to assume that only one settlement existed then. 'Gidding', for example, has five separate entries in Domesday Book but makes no reference to Little and Steeple Gidding. Little Gidding can, however, be identified with the holding of William 'inganie', or the Artificer, who had acquired the manor that Bricteva had held before the Norman Conquest. Steeple Gidding does not appear until the twelfth century when a Northamptonshire-style stone spire was erected over its tiny church, but it too has been identified with a Domesday manor of seven hides.

Early boundaries

The Anglo-Saxon period sees the beginning of the recording of boundaries in the form of land charters. Hundreds of these charters survive, some of them from an early seventh-century date but the majority from the ninth and tenth centuries. They record grants of land to laymen and monastic communities. In some cases the charter is merely a confirmation of an earlier grant, much as we see in later confirmations of medieval market charters by various kings of England. For Bedfordshire and Huntingdonshire several dozen charters survive but only a few are of value for tracing estate boundaries in the field. Many charters refer only to 'land at . . .' without describing the bounds. In other cases the estate boundary has been described in terms of features of the landscape that have not survived, such as trees, hedges, and areas of woodland.

Where the bounds are clearly set down and can be followed in the modern landscape there is a remarkable correlation of many of these Old English estates with the present parish boundaries, revealing the great antiquity and permanence of the parishes of the rural areas. Sometimes the civil parish no longer coincides with the ecclesiastical parish, but in practically all cases remote from the towns the former have been created by an amalgamation of the latter. Reference to the highly detailed tithe maps of the mid-nineteenth century will confirm that rural parish boundaries have remained unchanged over large areas of the two counties in recent decades once amalgamation has been taken into account.

The boundaries of the land charter covering the parish of Chalgrave in Bedfordshire (Fig. 5) were traced by F. G. Gurney in 1920.[4] The charter dates from A.D. 926 and it

[4] Gurney, F. G., 'Yttingaford and the tenth century bounds of Chalgrave and Linslade', *Bedfordshire Historical Record Society*, V, Part II (1920), pp. 161–179.

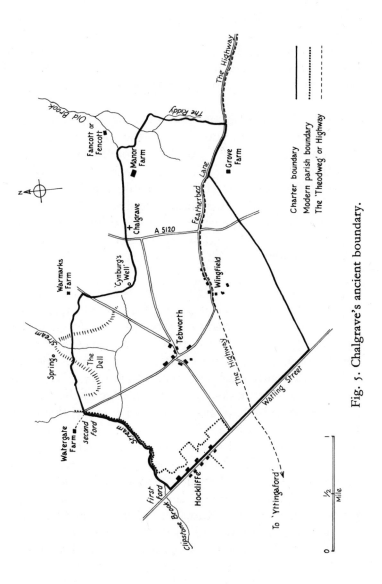

Fig. 5. Chalgrave's ancient boundary.

63

records a confirmation from Athelstan to his thane Ealdred of five hides of land, said to have been purchased from the 'heathen'. 'The heathen' doubtless refers to the Danes, whose influence had apparently spread further west than had been agreed at the Treaty of Wedmore in A.D. 878. The details of the charter are worth quoting in full:

Where the dyke shoots onto Watling Street, then along Watling Street till you come to the ford, then along the brook to the second ford. Then from the ford up to the spring, and thence to a dell, and then . . . to a dyke . . . and to the second dyke to the brook, and from the brook to Cynburg well. Then along the dyke to Eastcotan, . . . to the Old Brook, thence along the rithig. Then straight to the Highway [Theodweg] and along to the dyke, and along the dyke to Watling Street.

Most charters describe their bounds in a clockwise direction and this one is no exception. Watling Street, an unequivocal landmark, still forms a straight boundary for a mile on the western side of the parish and is mentioned at the beginning and end of the charter's description. The 'dyke' that 'shoots onto Watling Street' can still be recognised as a long ditch that marks the southern edge of the parish for over a mile and a half. For much of its length this ditch is still followed by a footpath. Northwards along the Roman road the boundary of this Saxon estate is lost in the street-village of Hockliffe. The village is not mentioned in Domesday Book although 'Hocgan clif' does appear in an earlier eleventh-century document. It seems unlikely that there was any settlement on the Roman road when the charter was compiled otherwise there is little doubt that it would have been recorded. Hence the first ford mentioned would have been reached by going eastwards from a deserted road, probably where the present Woburn road, the A50, crosses the Clipstone Brook. The brook should then be followed upstream for a mile to where another ford still exists at the crossing of a track from Tebworth close to Watergate Farm. On the west side of the brook the trackway continues as a bridleway. The estate boundary is then difficult to trace across undulating farmland. The 'dell', however, is almost certainly the small valley that lies due north of Tebworth separating the farms of Watergate and Warmarks. A number of springs emerge from the edge of the Chalk in this area and one of these forms the next distinctive point in this thousand-year-old charter as Cynburg's Well. The well is really a spring, now known as Kimberwell. The name commemorates St Cyneburh, daughter of the heathen king of Mercia, Penda. Cyneburh had been converted through her marriage to Alchfrid, the son of Oswy, the Christian king of Northumbria, and had founded a convent at Castor in the Soke of Peterborough. The church there still bears the dedication to St Kyneburga. Upon her death in A.D. 680 a cult developed from her life and death and it would appear that the spring at Chalgrave had been attributed with healing powers in her name. Gurney relates that even in living memory people had resorted to the well for a cure for their weak eyes.

From the well the boundary continues towards Chalgrave church which has an eccentric position on the extreme northern boundary of the parish. Here, it is believed, lay the 'Eastcotan' of the charter. Although that name is now lost, a closely related place-name Fancott can still be found, in a marshy bottom just over the boundary in Toddington parish. This is likely to have been the cottage in the fen, just as Eastcotan was the settlement on the eastern side of Chalgrave parish. The 'Old Brook' of the charter also survives in name and location, running along the parish boundary eastwards from the church. From there the estate boundary turned south along a stream, the 'rithig' or riddy being a local term for a small stream, and reached the Highway or theodweg as the charter terms it. This was not the Roman road, mentioned at the beginning of the charter, but part of a long trackway that Gurney identified as an ancient cross-country route. In Chalgrave it is known as Featherbed Lane and can be followed in part from its junction with the A5120 road and the minor road to Wingfield. The estate boundary only followed it for a short distance, however, taking a left fork just north of Grove Farm, Houghton Regis, and picking up the long dike or ditch that began the estate bounds until Watling Street is reached again. Here then is a parish boundary that has survived unchanged for over a thousand years and along which those features described in the land charter can still be recognised in the landscape. Another tenth-century description of bounds survives for west Bedfordshire where some of the topographic features can still be recognised. The charter for Asplea (Aspley Guise) in A.D. 969 is less clear than that for Chalgrave although the details it provides are as extensive:

> From Hysse Burn [Husborne Crawley] to Wendlesdun [Wensdon Hill], eastward from Wendlesdun to Flitan Hyll, thence on to the white moor afterwards by a fen to the chief field . . . thence to the apple tree where the boundaries meet, of the men of Woburn and the men of Wafandun [Wavendon] and of the men of Aepslea [Aspley]. From the deer gate over the heath to the combe then round West Lea. From the lea to the chief field which is on the boundary of the men of Aepslea and Wafandun . . .

Thus runs the first part of the description. Wensdon Hill is a clear starting-point, located mid-way between Church End, Husborne Crawley and the village of Aspley Guise, and from the route which follows it is clear that a clockwise direction was intended as it heads across the infertile sands of Aspley Heath. There is now a separate parish of that name but it was formerly part of Woburn Sands. Even earlier it formed part of Wavendon and the name Old

Wavendon Heath can still be found on the 2½″ Ordnance Survey map of the area. Hence the meeting of the boundaries of the men of Woburn, Wavendon and Aspley, no longer possible but probably located where Aspley Lane meets the A50 road. From there the estate boundary ran across the heath and although the area is now covered in woodland something of the wasteland which once existed can still be discerned in this, one of the most attractive parts of modern Bedfordshire. From the heath the boundary followed the 'West Lea', the stream that rises from a spring just south of Mill Farm and north of the village of Woburn Sands. But perhaps the clearest feature, and one of the most exciting parts of the itinerary for the local historian, is the next point of the description where the record shows that the waste between Aspley and Wavendon had already gone and the boundary lay along one of the great open fields of Aspley. This open field can be traced from estate maps of the eighteenth century which reveal the pre-enclosure landscape, the furlongs and strips drawn like a patchwork quilt across much of the parish. The map of 1745[5] shows blocks of furlongs at right angles to one another in the Crabtree Farm area of the parish, the strips abutting onto the parish boundary with Wavendon. This has produced an irregular boundary but one which follows precisely the old open field in a stepped effect, with sharp right-angled bends. In 1760 the fields of Apsley were enclosed, but the line of the boundary was of course immovable, preserving in the landscape not only a reminder of the pre-enclosure landscape but, given the details of the land charter, the line of an Old English estate boundary (see Fig. 6).

North of the field the charter is much more difficult to trace on the ground for the description goes beyond Aspley Guise and into Salford parish. But it would appear that the Saxon estate embraced the hamlet of Holcot—now part of the joint parish of Holcot and Salford—for the charter refers

[5] B.R.O. X1/30.

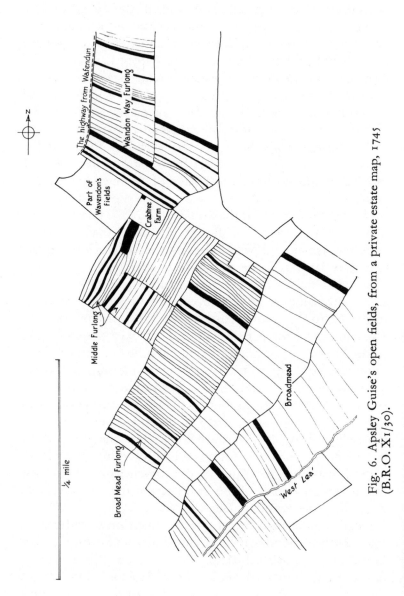

Fig. 6. Apsley Guise's open fields, from a private estate map, 1745 (B.R.O. X1/30).

to another meeting point of several estates. This was the northern limit of the *Aesplea* estate, where it abutted upon the land of the 'men of *Cranefeld* [Cranfield] and the men of *Mereston* [Marston Moretaine]'. Holcot is mentioned but there is no separate reference to the men of the hamlet and it is likely, therefore, that it formed part of the estate. It is interesting to note that the meeting point lay in woodland for there is mention of an old charcoal pit. The present location of the meeting place of the three boundaries is a remote corner at the north-eastern end of Holcot Wood. Close by lies the hamlet of Cranfield's Wood End and an isolated moated site pinpoints the first settlement in that area. Wood End was Wodende when it was first recorded in A.D. 1250. The charter also makes reference to the 'long corner' which the boundary followed after its junction near Wood End. We notice that Holcot Wood still makes a long, narrow pan-handle between Cranfield, Marston Moretaine and Ridgmont parishes.

Huntingdonshire is better served than Bedfordshire when it comes to reliable modern studies of early Anglo-Saxon charters, for the county is among those that have been covered by the scholarly hand of Dr C. R. Hart.[6] Several of the charters reveal once more the great permanence of these pre-Norman boundaries. Haddon, Alwalton and perhaps Conington with Holme have their present bounds along at least part of the ancient lines. Haddon is worth looking at in a little more detail, for the simplicity of its bounds if nothing else. The Old English estate was described in a confirmation charter by King Eadred to his thane Ælfsige in A.D. 951:

First from Ermine Street to Somerledsditch . . . to Billing-brook . . . north along the brook to the landmark . . . along the way to the old ditch, east along the ditch to the elder tree stump and on to the street, south along the street until Somerledsditch.

[6] Hart, C. R., *The Early Charters of Eastern England* (1966).

The present parish forms a rectangle whose eastern boundary is clearly defined along the Roman road of Ermine Street. On the southern edge it follows a brook, which we may take to be Somerledsditch, and then continues due west for a mile before reaching the Billing Brook. The course of the boundary is then easily followed northwards along the stream until it turns east and picks up a large ditch for half a mile at Haddon Lodge. The elder tree stump has long since vanished but the ditch remains, and soon we are back onto *the street*. Dr M. D. Hooper has investigated the botanical evidence from the hedges that still coincide with the charter boundary, and through the use of his hedgerow dating technique has found them to be as old, at least, as the charter. In a county where very few hedges pre-date the parliamentary enclosures of the eighteenth century this is an interesting survival which must owe its existence to the long established boundary along whose length the hedges lie. The hedges of nearby Conington, where a charter survives for A.D. 957, produced similar evidence of considerable antiquity.[7]

In some cases, even where the bounds are given, it is still not possible to trace the line as described in the charter because part of the estate lay in the fen. The foundation charter for the monastery at Peterborough, which describes the land given by Wulfhere, King of the Mercians, in A.D. 664, refers to land in northern Huntingdonshire, including all the 'meres and fen' but the details are too vague to be of value to a field worker in the twentieth century. But one place in the old record seems to be recognisable through the mists of time. *Scælfremere* is mentioned and we may identify that with Chalderbeach Farm, deep in the fen of Holme. Similarly, a charter describing the bounds of Yaxley and Farcet is vague as they involved substantial areas of fenland. One suspects that if the charters were more numerous or their detail greater then the number of rural

[7] Hooper, M. D., *Hedges and Local History* (1971).

parishes where boundaries have remained undisturbed for more than a thousand years would be substantially increased.

In some parts of rural England the boundaries of the Saxon hundreds have also been recognised as significant landscape features, whether they be followed by an earthen bank, a green lane or minor metalled road, their line continuous over a number of miles. Unfortunately, the hundreds of Bedfordshire and Huntingdonshire are not easily recognised in the landscape. The lines that may be drawn on a map follow parish boundaries but are only to be found as bridleways or footpaths in short, discontinuous stretches or an occasional piece of green lane. The present hundreds are not the same as those that existed in Saxon times for some have disappeared and others have amalgamated. Domesday Huntingdonshire, for example, mentions a rather curious Kimbolton Hundred in 1066 but which had apparently been absorbed into Leightonstone by 1086. At Gidding, also in the Hundred of Leightonstone, land was said to be formerly in the Hundred of Cresswell but there is no other mention of this mysterious Saxon hundred.

But if the present boundaries are themselves a disappointment in the present landscape the meeting places of a number of the hundreds make interesting objects of personal exploration in the field and a number can be tracked down on the ground. At these meeting places the hundred court was held, and the men of the hundred were expected to attend to hear cases of petty crime and misdemeanours. Such courts met, so we are led to believe, in the open air and the recognition of their sites certainly shows a strong preference for the countryside, avoiding towns and villages. Wherever possible the meeting place was central to the hundred and this principle can sometimes be useful in locating an uncertain site.

Huntingdonshire's four hundreds present few problems. Norman Cross Hundred, the more northerly of the four, probably had an earlier Saxon name before its present

Danish one. There was no Domesday settlement of Norman Cross and even today the place is only peopled by those who serve the travellers on the Great North Road, the A1, for it lies at the junction of that road and the A15 to Peterborough. The place was sufficiently isolated in the Napoleonic Wars for the government of the day to establish a large prisoner-of-war camp for captured French soldiers and seamen. A pillar surmounted by an eagle commemorates the camp just north of the cross-roads on the A1 and on the A15 stands the rather severe three-storied frontage of the late Georgian house that the prisoners built for the camp commandant. Of the other hundreds, Toseland and Hurstingstone both had meeting places that were probably empty of settlement in the eleventh century. Toseland takes its name from the Scandinavian 'Toli's grove' and although there is now a village of that name none was mentioned in Domesday. Hurstingstone, that most wooded of the hundreds, had its meeting place or moot at Woodhurst. The last of the four, Leightonstone, takes its name, like Hurstingstone, from an actual stone that marked the location of the court. Leighton Bromswold is recorded in Domesday Book but the meeting place appears to have been some distance north of the church for a large stone has recently been recovered from the fields in that area and now stands by the lychgate of the church (Plate 4).

Bedfordshire hundred meeting places are not so easy to locate because a number are no longer represented by place-names in common usage. Manshead Hundred, for example, cannot be connected with any contemporary settlement. But a careful examination of an eighteenth-century estate map for Eversholt reveals a number of fields and closes that bear the name—Great and Little Manshead Close, Manshead Path Furlong and Manshead Field.[8] The fields lie on the boundary with Tingrith parish and accord well with the derivation of that place-name as 'assembly stream'. Another

[8] B.R.O. R1/248.

document, an early seventeenth-century glebe terrier, betrays the location of Stodden Hundred's meeting place for it refers to 'Stodden Fields' on the western edge of the open fields of Pertenhall.[9] Deadman's Oak, at the southern end of Sheerhatch Wood, Willington, is traditionally associated with the meeting place of Wixamtree Hundred as it lies central to the Hundred and a number of tracks and footpaths radiate from it.

A Christian country

The history of the early Christian church in Bedfordshire and Huntingdonshire remains an uncharted story. Surviving Saxon documents are not much concerned with its affairs. Between the hoard of late Roman Christian silver recovered from the site of Durobrivae and the establishment of monastic communities in the fens during the seventh century there is a long silence. The dedication of the church at Colne to St Helen provides some evidence that this was not entirely a heathen interlude. One wonders what had happened at Water Newton, scarcely a stone's throw from the walls of an important Roman town, shortly after the Roman withdrawal for the church dedication to St Remigius is no less remarkable than that of Colne. St Remigius is another of the very early saints of the new church that was spreading westwards from Rome. He had been a fifth-century bishop of Gaulish descent who was said to have evangelised the Franks. Can the dedication at Water Newton relate to some survival of Christianity at Durobrivae or was he one of the saints imported by the new settlers? In view of the date at which Remigius was active it seems more likely that the latter was the case.

Whether the sub-Roman church survived for long will remain problematic, but certainly by the mid-seventh cen-

[9] Emmison, F. G., 'The meeting places of Stodden and Redbournstoke Hundreds', *Bedfordshire Historical Record Society*, XII (1928).

tury the two counties would have been involved in a strong religious revival. Bede records the establishment of a monastery at Medeshamsted, where St Peter's church was later to change the name to Peterborough, and it is certain that northern Huntingdonshire came under its influence. The Soke of Peterborough is particularly rich in late Saxon churches but Bedfordshire and Huntingdonshire are less well off. Not until the eve of the Norman Conquest can dates be ascribed to church buildings and even then only a dozen or so can be visited. The poor building stone of most of the two counties might well be to blame for this paucity for those that do survive lie close to the rivers that enabled the import of good building stone. A fine stone frieze at Fletton preserves the finest example of Anglo-Saxon art. It has been dated to the first half of the ninth century, but the pink colouring of the stone leads Professor Pevsner to suspect that this is a piece of work imported whole from nearby Peterborough. The monastery there was damaged by fire in A.D. 1116 and the frieze was probably rescued from the ruins and transported across the Nene to Fletton. A more genuine Saxon church lies at Great Paxton, close to the River Ouse. The cruciform plan was created about A.D. 1020 and it is perhaps unique for the quality of Saxon workmanship and the similarity it bears to a number of churches elsewhere in Western Europe.

Great Paxton would have been a minister church, a church with a clerical establishment serving a large area and several settlements before the setting up of parish churches in every village. These minster churches had several clergy attached to them. Our knowledge of the minsters in the two counties is most fragmentary but when the church of St Paul, Bedford, was described in Domesday Book two secular canons were serving the church, the remnant of an earlier community of monks of a minster church. The place-name of Maulden, in central Bedfordshire, is instructive for it is derived from the 'cross on the hill'. The existing church stands on the brow of a hill overlooking the village and separate from it—although uneven ground to the north suggests that there may once have been buildings close by— and a small piece of stone on the open ground to the east marks the site of a cross. Was this lofty site, in the centre of the Lower Greensand and commanding extensive views to the south, the location of one of those first churches, where a cross marked the place of an open air meeting?

By the eleventh century most of the main settlements had acquired their own churches. Fifty-two places are recorded in Huntingdonshire as possessing at least one church and in some cases several were recorded. Huntingdon, St Ives, Stukeley and Hartford had two each—although in Stukeley's case this is likely to be explained by the existence of Great and Little Stukeley—and Sawtry had three. Even today, Sawtry has two churches although one of them, St Andrew, has little remaining above ground. Its derelict churchyard lies to the east of the dual carriageway of the A1. Once it stood on the Great North Road, before modern improvements diverted the busy traffic. The third church was at Sawtry Judith, the manor held by Countess Judith, niece to William the Conqueror. The record of churches in the Domesday folios for Bedfordshire is far from complete. The scribes chose only to record those at Bedford and on the royal manors of Leighton, Luton and Houghton Regis. Other churches were certainly in existence by that date and in some the evidence of Saxon architecture is visible. For instance, in the south of the county Caddington has the remains of characteristic long and short work in the western end of its narrow nave, and at Clapham the tower is solid Saxon apart from its Norman top. Yet Clapham church was only a chapel of ease to the nearby mother church at Oakley in the early part of the Middle Ages. Although there is little documentary evidence for Saxon Oakley, and no visible Saxon architecture, the fact that the monks of Ramsey held land there in A.D. 988 suggests that a church was already in

existence. It may well have been an early foundation if
Clapham has developed from it. Elsewhere in Bedfordshire,
but recorded in the Domesday account for Hertfordshire,
a priest was mentioned at Barwythe, which we can identify
as Barworth in Studham parish. It is not absolutely certain
that there was a church at Barworth for when William de
Eltesdun was granted a licence for a chapel at Barworth in
A.D. 1236 he had to give a pledge that it would not infringe
upon the rights of the mother church at Studham. At Everton, both a priest and a church were mentioned in the
Huntingdonshire folios but the parish now lies in Bedfordshire.

Quite a number of the early medieval churches were in
reality chapels of ease to an older mother church, an attach-
ment that some were unable to shake off until the nineteenth
century. In most cases the mother churches are to be found
in the larger villages, such as Somersham, Huntingdonshire,
where the church had control over those at Colne and Pidley,
two of the constituent members of the Somersham Soke.
Yet it must be remembered Colne's dedication to St Helen
suggests the presence there of a church at an early date.
Land at Somersham had long been part of the endowment
of the seventh-century monastery of Ely and the Ely bishops
were later to build a large summer palace there. Other
chapels of ease are perhaps more surprising. Silsoe, for
example, remained in that condition until 1831 in spite of
standing at the entrance to the house of one of Bedfordshire's oldest and most influential families, the de Greys of
Wrest Park. The memorials to past de Greys lie in the
mother church of Flitton, one and a half miles away.

The Dark Ages closed on a landscape that had undergone
considerable change since the Romans had withdrawn over
six hundred years before. The countryside was filling up
with new villages and farms and the areas of waste must
have already dwindled to a few patches on the most marginal
of land over large areas of the two counties. But in parts

primeval woodland was still extensive and it awaited clearance and colonisation in the early Middle Ages. Domesday Book makes it plain that by the twelfth century cultivated land would have been the most obvious feature of the landscape. New urban centres were beginning to emerge, but we still know all too little about the origins of the small towns of England, while others awaited the efforts of speculators in the prosperous years of the thirteenth century. This prosperity was to witness the last great phase of woodland clearance and it is to that process that we should next turn our attention.

SELECT BIBLIOGRAPHY

Bond, F., *Dedications and Patron Saints of English Churches* (1914).
Hart, C. R., *The Early Charters of Eastern England* (1966).
Mawer, A. and Stenton, F. M., *The Place-Names of Bedfordshire and Huntingdonshire; English Place-Name Society,* Vol III (1926).
Morris, J. (Ed.), *Domesday Book: 19—Huntingdonshire* (1975).
The Victoria History of the County of Bedford, Vol. I (1904) and
The Victoria History of the County of Huntingdonshire, Vol. I (1926).
Pevsner, N., *The Buildings of England—Bedfordshire and Huntingdonshire* (1968).

3. Medieval expansion and colonisation

The clearance of the medieval woodland. Deer parks. Castle, town, village and farm in the landscape.

The clearance of the medieval woodland

THE EVIDENCE OF Domesday Book suggests that only the Lower Greensand in Bedfordshire and Hurstingstone Hundred in eastern Huntingdonshire had substantial areas of ancient woodland remaining at the close of the eleventh century. Elsewhere, we may conclude that much woodland had already been cleared before records began in the twelfth century, and this conclusion is borne out by the early medieval records that mention the surviving great woods.

The best evidence for the state of woodland in the two counties comes from Huntingdonshire, where there were several royal 'forests'. The whole of the county lay under Forest Law between 1155 and 1300. This does not mean that the whole of Huntingdonshire was an unbroken woodland wilderness or that the hunting rights of the Crown—which the laws were to protect—prevented most villages from cultivating the land as they had done before. Successive English kings used the designation of large tracts of the country as 'Royal Forest' as a method of increasing revenue, for anyone who wished to fell trees and extend their area of cultivation would be expected to pay handsomely for the licence that was required. Only occasionally would a county under such restrictive laws see a royal hunting party and even then they would have had a preference for particular locations. Three such locations can be recognised in central Huntingdonshire, all within a convenient distance of the town of Huntingdon. They were the Forests of Harthay,

Weybridge and Sapley. They formed part of a much larger area of woodland that stretched across mid-county from Coppingford in the west to Somersham in the east. Fragments of the old woods still survive here and the hedgerows are thick with mature oaks.

Already at the time of the Domesday Survey Harthay Forest belonged to the Crown, and it is likely that the other two woods were already royal properties in 1086. The countryside of Harthay Forest is now almost empty of trees but the name is remembered in the farms of High and Low Harthay. To the south, however, there still stands the ancient wood of Brampton Wood—which was not part of Harthay Forest despite the claims made upon it by the Crown—and which is now managed by the Forestry Commission. Fortunately it is open to the public on certain days of the week. Brampton Wood features in a description of the bounds of Harthay which were documented in 1154–55 when the whole of the county came under Forest Law. The description is repeated in 1300 at the time of the disafforestation. By the later date Brampton Wood was no longer Crown land for it passed to the bishops of Ely in 1215, although it had earlier received visits from King John, Stephen, Henry I, II and III. The description of the bounds is of interest for the mention that is made of a lost hamlet:

From Houtoneslinche between the field of Houghton and cover of the said wood [Harthay] as far as Brampton Wood and so by the bounds of the same wood from Brampton to Hertheye to the field of Sybethorpe and so between the said field and the cover of Hertheye as far as Rokespol and so to the duct ascending to Wykenland.

The bounds begin on the north-eastern side of the forest, probably not far from the junction of the A1 road with the A604 and west of the motel of Brampton Hut. The 'linche' of 'Houtone' is no longer traceable because the fields in this area have undergone considerable change both during the eighteenth century and in the past few decades but the bank must have run southwards from the Ellington Brook. An estate map locates for us the former hamlet of Houtone or Houghton[1] in the names of a group of fields—all now gone with the reorganisation of parliamentary enclosure—that lay just west of Grove Farm. 'Houghton Closes', 'Houghton Ploughed Close', 'Houghton Corner' and 'Great Houghton Close' lay on either side of a track that widened out along a dog-leg bend. Fragments of woodland are shown on the map, particularly to the west. It seems certain that these closes identify the location of the hamlet, a tiny settlement of which nothing else is known. These remaining patches of woodland also indicate the approximate line of the forest bounds 'between the field of Houghton'. Brampton Wood, which is mentioned next, has probably changed little from its Domesday extent, when it was said to be half a league in length and two furlongs in width. If anything it has increased in width, but it has certainly remained unchanged for the past two hundred years. Its present northern boundary, where it abutted upon Harthay, would be little different from that existing in the eleventh and twelfth centuries.

The name Sybethorpe in this medieval description poses few problems even though it is no longer to be found in the landscape. It can be identified from John Speed's county map of 1610 as a hamlet just to the south of Ellington, where Ellington Thorpe now lies. A moated site at Thorpe Lodge certainly helps in locating this lost medieval settlement. The 'field of Sybethorpe' might also be identified in the long narrow fields that can be seen south and east of the hamlet. Their slightly curving boundaries suggest that they were formerly part of a large open field. To the south of the long narrow fields the pattern of enclosure changes. There the fields are more irregular in outline and size and it is probable that they represent part of the onslaught of clearance that

[1] Map by Dumbleton and Hall, 1772. H.R.O. SF 452.

Plate 1 Maiden Bower. Much of the oval outline of the Neolithic causewayed camp still survives—overlain by the rampart of a later Iron Age fort—although chalk quarrying has damaged one side. A mile to the south runs the prehistoric Icknield Way.

Plate 2 This remarkable aerial photograph reveals a regular grid of small fields, bounded by ditches, on the rich soils of the Ivel Valley at Northill. The area is noted for its abundance of Roman finds and the orientation of these forgotten fields is still followed by roads and tracks nearby.

Plate 3 The raised line of a Roman road at Old Warden is accentuated by the shallow ditches on either side. This road ran from Shefford to a large Roman-British settlement between Cople and Willington.

Plate 4 The hundred stone at Leighton Bromswold. In some parts of the country such stones marked the meeting place of the Saxon hundred. Unearthed some years ago in fields to the north-east of the parish church, it now lies by the lychgate.

Plate 5 Old Warden Abbey. Although practically nothing of this Cistercian house survives above ground, aerial photography reveals a complex pattern of walls and fishponds. The sixteenth-century mansion John Gostwick built on the site has also gone, apart from the gate-house isolated amidst the fields.

Plate 6 Knotting Manor in 1646. One of the few early estate maps to be made for northern Bedfordshire, it shows substantial areas of woodland on the eastern boundary with Melchbourne and Riseley, all since cleared. The small closes in the south-east contain several 'stocking' names.

Plate 7 The huge moat at Park Farm, Eaton Bray, and the disturbed ground within it, marks the site of William de Cantlowe's manor house, built in 1221. The moat was first mentioned in 1273 when a drawbridge allowed access into the deer park.

Plate 8 Yielden Castle. The great earthen mound and ramparts of the Norman motte and bailey castle built by Geoffrey de Trailly form one of the most spectacular features of medieval Bedfordshire. Beyond the bailey can be seen the house plots and lanes of the former village that sheltered under the castle's walls.

Plate 9 Cainhoe Castle with its deserted village. One of the most impregnable of Bedfordshire's medieval castles, there is strong evidence to suggest that its village was wiped out by the Black Death.

Plate 10 The plantation town of Kimbolton was centred upon the wide market place, whose establishment in the year 1200 involved the diversion of the main road in order to collect tolls on market days. Kimbolton Castle, rebuilt by Vanbrugh, now dominates the eastern end of the town. Its medieval predecessor stood further away.

Plate 11 St Ives. The town hugs the bank of the River Ouse downstream from the church that once served the hamlet of Slepe, for the river was the source of prosperity and trade in the Middle Ages. The fifteenth-century bridge brought travellers straight into the long market place, where both weekly market and annual fair were held.

Plate 12 Chellington deserted village. Bedfordshire's lost villages are poorly represented on the surface as a result of modern ploughing, but Chellington has survived in the irregular pasture field below the church. Part of the former open fields can also be seen in the ridge-and-furrow.

Plate 13 Biddenham Church End. The bulk of the present village lies half a mile away around a pretty green, but this aerial photograph shows that part of the village once lay between the church and the River Ouse.

was made on the forest at some time during the Middle Ages, a time that may well have been soon after the Crown had abandoned their hunting interest. It was the men of Ellington who had suffered at the time of the Norman Conquest for their ten hide manor had been reduced to nine by William, or as Domesday Book records 'on account of the King's woodland'.

Harthay is not among the enclosed deer parks that Christopher Saxton chose to include on his fine county map of 1576, which is some indication that it had already disappeared. Weybridge is included, however, and it remained Crown property until the end of the sixteenth century. By then, however, it must have been considerably smaller than four hundred years earlier for the Crown had been content to licence out or give permission for part of it to be cleared. In 1259, for example, Henry II had given fifty acres of assarts to Merton Priory in Surrey with leave to make further assarts and to cultivate part of the forest. That which survived into the sixteenth century as hunting forest was leased to the warden, Sir Richard Cromwell, in 1542. One condition of the lease was the maintaining of at least one hundred deer. In the early years of the next century the Crown at last relinquished its hold on the forest and the Cromwells became owners. They soon sold to Edward, Viscount Mandeville, whose residence lay at Kimbolton, but even then there was a covenant attached which required six hundred bucks and does to be kept in the forest, and it was not until the expiry of the covenant in 1660 that the remnant of the medieval woodland could be cleared.

Sapley was probably cleared of most of its woodland by the end of the fourteenth century although it too is one of Saxton's deer parks—most likely a small area centred on Sapley Park Farm—and although the clearance is not documented the evidence of the landscape is clearer than in the case of either Harthay or Weybridge. Around Sapley Park Farm and 'The Moat' that lies half a mile to the north is a group of small fields with twisting, irregular boundaries made up of broad and varied hedgerows. A considerable number have unfortunately been removed in recent years but sufficient survive to reveal an area of early medieval woodland clearance. The minor roads running north from Huntingdon to Abbots Ripton and Kings Ripton circumscribe this landscape in making a large U-shaped curve north of the present hamlet of Sapley. The botanical evidence from the hedges on either side of the roads has shown them to be parts of former woodland, relic features left when the wood was cut down in the early Middle Ages.

The clearance of two of the three royal forests during the Middle Ages reveals that at least one part of Huntingdonshire had not been empty of woodland at the time Domesday Book was compiled. But it should be emphasised that these forests were minor elements in the landscape and represented a very small portion of the county in the twelfth and thirteenth centuries. Even if we include the tracts of woodland that lay outside the properties of the Crown the impression is still one of a largely open landscape. The remaining woodland was contiguous with the three Crown forests and fragments survive in Monks Wood, Bevills Wood and Warboys Wood, together with several smaller areas scattered between Sawtry and Somersham. Monks and Bevills Wood are only parted by a minor road for a short distance and together form the largest area of ancient woodland remaining in Huntingdonshire, the former being the centre of an experimental station where a great amount of botanical research on hedgerow dating has been accomplished. The history of Monks Wood also has the advantage of being well documented. It formed part of the Domesday estate of the Countess Judith, known in later years as Sawtry Judith Manor. In 1086 the wood was part of a larger tract of forest that encompassed Ewingeswood (later Monks) and Little Wood (later Archers Wood and still to be seen behind the earthworks of the manor site), in extent eighteen furlongs by four. The manor formed part of the endowment of the Cistercian monastery at Sawtry in 1147 and the documents reveal that the wood was enclosed. King John gave further permission in 1205 for the wood's enclosure and in 1242 the monks were allowed to cut a trench or hollow way for the better protection of travellers through the forest—remembering that the whole of the county was still under forest law and permission would be necessary. Part of the original hedge line that enclosed the wood can be recognised from an aerial photograph of the southern area. A few yards west of the point where the minor road emerges from its narrow route through the dense woodland of Monks and Bevills, and between the road and Monks Wood, the fields are regular in outline but the photograph reveals a twisting hedge-bank crossing the area. A detailed estate map of Sawtry in 1612[2] shows the woodland to be half as big again at that time and it is likely that it stretched down to the hedge-bank (see Fig. 7). As the bank follows the line of the hundred boundary it is almost certainly the very same feature that occurs in the twelfth century description. During the seventeenth or eighteenth century the wood was cut back to its present position and the hedge-bank left as a piece of relic woodland and a field boundary, which has itself been discarded by further reorganisation of the fields.

The work on the Monks Wood hedge has been carried out by Dr Pollard and his investigation of other relic hedges that were once part of an area of woodland in the county provide one method of locating where most of the clearances were being made in the early part of the Middle Ages. Many hedges have been destroyed in the Huntingdonshire countryside in recent years but Dr Pollard was still able to investigate over two hundred hedges. The greatest number of ancient relic woodland hedges were to be found in Hurstingstone Hundred and westwards into the centre of the county while a second area could be recognised in the

[2] H.R.O. PM 4/6a.

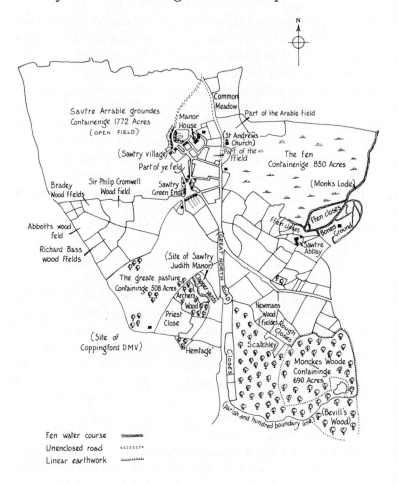

Fen water course
Unenclosed road
Linear earthwork

Fig. 7. The parishes of Sawtry All Saints and Sawtry St Andrew, 1612 (H.R.O. PM 4/6A).

south-west, along the Bedfordshire border.[3] Hedges are a source of landscape evidence that is under constant threat of destruction and by itself the counting of plant species cannot be considered sufficiently precise or detailed a method for identifying medieval clearances. Indeed, the high intensity of the arable agriculture that is currently practised over much of the two counties has contributed to the obliteration of medieval landscape features; today there are few traces of the small irregular fields that were often the result of woodland clearance five hundred years ago. One clear exception can be seen in a remote part of Turvey parish where it borders with Stevington and Carlton. Great Oaks Wood is the last remnant of an ancient forest that once stretched over a large part of the area and there are several clumps of woodland together with massive hedge-banks scattered amongst a landscape of small and irregular shaped fields. Unfortunately there are no documents to trace out the evolution of this ancient tract of woodland, only the silent inexplicable features of the present landscape remain. A similar example occurs at Cranfield where there is documentary evidence of clearance taking place but here the details are far too vague to read in the topography of the modern parish. Nevertheless the small fields that lie on the ridge top beyond East End, and where some woodland still survives, can be nothing else but part of that medieval phase of woodland clearance.

The documentary sources that describe the felling of woodland—the process sometimes referred to in the Norman-French term of 'assarting'—are both variable in their detail and in the parts of the two counties that are covered. Most relate to land held by monasteries and with the great rise in the number of such institutions during the twelfth and thirteenth centuries it is useful to strike a note of caution here. The economy of the monastic estates was

[3] Pollard, E., 'Hedges VII: woodland relic hedges in Huntingdon and Peterborough', *Journal of Ecology,* 61, No. 2 (1973), pp. 343–52.

recorded in detail and preserved down the centuries; in contrast the work of lay lords was often left without documentary record. Consequently, the great religious communities, through the abundant evidence that has come down to us through monastic cartularies, seem to play an overwhelming part in rolling back the medieval forest frontier. The sharp increase in the volume of sources is also something to treat with care for the knowledge of woodland clearances that can be gleaned from them could prompt the assumption that there was a massive onslaught on the wastes simply because there are no earlier documents than Domesday Book to point to clearances during the Dark Ages. If the documentation of twelfth and thirteenth century Bedfordshire is looked at in some detail, for example, a picture is built up of small-scale clearances, many of only a few acres at a time, which overall do not amount to a major attack on the wastes but a piece-meal tidying-up process of the remaining woodland on the more marginal land, a response to the growing demands of an expanding population that had already reached the point where the good soils were cleared and under cultivation. It is only in the more marginal locations that woodland clearance can be regarded as an important theme in the development of the medieval landscape of this part of England.

A number of monastic cartularies provide details of the endowment of the various houses that held property in the two counties. The cartulary for the Cistercian monastery at Old Warden is probably the most instructive. When the order was established here by Walter Espec in A.D. 1135 a site was chosen in the west of the parish. The Cistercians— the new order of white monks—had earned respect for their emphasis on self denial and devotion to prayer. As an order they chose privacy and seclusion. We can therefore assume that the site in Old Warden (see Plate 5) was well isolated from any settlement. It was over three miles from the river gravels of the River Ivel where we have already recognised a landscape occupied since Roman times. The soils of the Lower Greensand around the monastery were poor, both dry and infertile, but it is evident that some clearance of woodland had already occurred before the monks arrived. Proof of an earlier episode of clearing occurs in the foundation charter for the monastery where it was described as the church of 'St Mary de Sartis' or the church of the clearing or assart. Much of the land that was given to the monks in the first fifty years of the life of the house was either of small assarts or of woodland on the Lower Greensand. Grants of woodland normally contained the grantor's permission to enclose and eventually clear for cultivation, but the giving of assarts reveals that clearances were often the result of efforts made by laymen. Again, it seems evident from the details of a manor held by the Ramsey monks at Cranfield in the middle of the twelfth century that those in possession of assarts, who were being required to pay an increased rental as a result, were the freeholders of the estate. John, son of Adam, was required to render an increase of five shillings because of the increase he had had from his assart. In all, some thirty men were paying a rent and the majority of them had some assart land.[4]

The monks of Old Warden were not the only ones to hold land on the marginal soils of the Lower Greensand. Dunstable Priory, for example, had a number of estates in central Bedfordshire around the growing market town of the same name that had been founded by Henry I astride one of the medieval routes to the north. Philippus de Flitta gave an assart to Dunstable Priory in the first half of the thirteenth century, the exact date is not clear from the cartulary. The land was taken from the south-western part of Flitton. This assart could only have been recent clearance from the woodland—a fact implicit in the name of Le Hangre recorded in the cartulary. Chicksands Priory also lay within the Green-

[4] For this and other examples see Hart, W. H. and Rev. Ponsonby A. Lyons, *Cartularium Monasterii de Rameseia*, Vol. I–III (1884–1893).

sand and this twelfth-century house of Gilbertine nuns must have been on some of the poorest soils of Bedfordshire, where woodland was still quite extensive and its management a valuable source of revenue. In 1323 timber was sent from Chicksands to help rebuild the great central tower of the monastery at Ely. The magnificent octagonal lantern that was erected above the ruins of tower and wrecked chancel stands today as a monument to the building zeal and skill of the medieval masons and carpenters but the massive oak beams that are the main support of the structure —sixty-four feet long and over three feet in width—are also a reminder of the whole trees that were sent from central Bedfordshire. The timber must have been transported by water for the Ivel runs close to the Chicksands estate and this in turn empties into the Great Ouse that gave a direct water route to Ely.

Away from the little hills of the Greensand escarpment the number of references to woodland and its clearance diminishes in the cartularies although the area of south-west Huntingdonshire that was revealed by Dr Pollard's researches and the adjoining claylands of north and west Bedfordshire do deserve mention. The Cistercians at Old Warden were granted land in Huntingdonshire and Bushmead Priory held a number of assarts on the border of the two counties. In the first years of their existence the Cistercians were given Midloe Wood by the Abbot of Ramsey; a century later the woodland had been cleared and a monastic grange established there. The monks appear to have been very active in that district for in 1154 they had received Ravenshoe Wood and that too had been cleared. In 1206 King John gave permission for nearby Perry Wood to be enclosed and cleared. Fragments of both Midloe and Perry Wood still survive, although today we must consider them as new plantations rather than relics of medieval woodland. We can still locate the site of the Cistercian grange at Midloe by the large moat around the farmhouse of the same name.

Part of the estate that the medieval monks held can be recognised in the description of Midloe Manor at the time of a sale in 1797. The manor comprised two farms, one of 256 acres (Midloe Grange) and another of 79 acres, together with Midloe Woods, all of which were said to be 'nearly extra-parochial'.[5] Both farms were bounded by a narrow stream on their north and east which is named as Monks Ditch on a map that is almost contemporary with the sale and would seem to mark the edge of the extra-parochial area.[6] The estate had altered little since the Manor and Grange had been received by the Crown from the Abbot of Warden Abbey in 1524.[7]

One of the largest areas of woodland clearance to be mentioned in the documents of the early medieval period concerns land given to the Knights Templar at Sharnbrook in 1199. The two hundred acres of *assart* can still be located in the landscape, despite the fact that the medieval field boundaries have disappeared as a result of parliamentary enclosure in the second half of the eighteenth century. A pre-enclosure estate map shows a number of small closes on the northern edge of the parish, between Temple Wood and Temple Spinney and named as Temple Closes.[8] There can be little doubt that these are the clearances from the forest first made in the twelfth century. Over the parish boundary where the Knights Templar had their assarts, in the parish of Knotting, estate maps provide another source of evidence of medieval clearances in the use of certain field-names. *Stocking, Redding* and *Ridding* are field names that show where a field has been created by the grubbing-up of woodland and it is noticeable that while they might be encountered in documents of the early medieval period their use as field-names appears to die out from the maps of the

[5] H.R.O., 24/7/2.
[6] H.R.O. SM17/170.
[7] H.R.O., 49/3/1.
[8] From a map of 1765–70. B.R.O. X1/7.

eighteenth century. Even where it can be demonstrated that
new fields have been created by the removal of woodland
in recent centuries, these field-names are absent. We must
therefore conclude that they were mainly used in the Middle
Ages and where we are able to locate them today it is not
unreasonable to take these names as evidence of medieval
clearance. Such is the case of Knotting where several maps
give proof of the removal of woods that once bordered the
parish on the south and east in the first half of the seventeenth century. The map of 1646[9] (Plate 6) shows a number
of closes in the south of the parish, where it bordered on
Sharnbrook, with the common characteristic of 'stockinge'
in their names. More of these names lay between Halsey
Wood and a greatly enlarged Knotting Green. By the late
eighteenth century some of the woodland had already been
removed and the 'stockinge' names were already dis-
appearing.[10]

The *stocking* names can be found quite frequently on the
maps that have survived for those areas of the two counties
where other evidence has already suggested that woodland
clearance was important in the early medieval period. At
Flitwick, for example, a map of 1717 shows a number of
'stocking' closes to the north and west of the church, lying
between the open fields of the manor and Flitwick Wood,
the latter having been mentioned in the early thirteenth
century part of the Dunstable Cartulary.[11] In fact, one of
the earliest mentions of such a field-name comes from that
same cartulary when the Prior received a grant of a *cultura,*
or area of plough-land, at Segenho (later to become Ridgmont parish), named '*Hamstockinge*' in the early thirteenth
century. The reference to a cultura at Segenho seems to
imply that the area cleared from the wood had not necessarily been enclosed and might well have formed part of the

[9] B.R.O. R1/254.
[10] A map for 1772. B.R.O. R1/46.
[11] B.R.O. LL17/338.

90

open fields of the manor. Although many of the clearances were the result of the activities of the rising class of freemen, it should not be assumed that their assarts always passed into individual ownership. Sometimes the freshly cleared land became part of the common fields. An undated grant of an assart at Coppingford makes this clear. The monks of Bushmead were given sixteen and a half selions of assart near to the hermitage and chapel at Coppingford, together with an area of woodland and the grant of free pannage for ten pigs. It is the word 'selions' that is significant for this was the term used to describe the strips of land that were the basis for ploughing the medieval open field. Such uses for assarts are not common, however, and the few examples that can be found are not easy to trace in the landscape. One other example can be seen on the pre-enclosure map for Husborne Crawley.[12] The parish was almost entirely in open field cultivation in the first part of the eighteenth century, apart from a few home closes around Church End and Husborne. But in the centre of the open fields was Stocking Hedge Furlong with no enclosed field of hedge to suggest that it alluded to a close that had since disappeared. Perhaps here was an area of assart that had been claimed by the expanding open field?

Although the evidence of the landscape, documents and maps is available to tell us something of the process of woodland clearance, the overall impression that is conveyed is that the two counties are by no means classic areas for such studies. In most parishes a general impression of the landscape in the twelfth and thirteenth centuries contains substantial areas of common open field with closes confined either to individual house plots in the village centre or on the outer edge of the parish adjacent to a small fragment of woodland from which they had been carved. Some parishes of course have a complex pattern of open field and closes amongst which are scattered a number of hamlets that have

12 B.R.O. R1/42.

come into being as a result of rather more extensive clearances; this is certainly the case at Cranfield and Eversholt, for example. The details of the operation of the open fields are obscure but one or two sources give us some insight and it is noticeable that they contain no references to assart or closes.

One of the earliest extant manorial court rolls concerns the Manor of Chalgrave—where the Saxon land charter has already been described—for the period 1278–1313.[13] The manor was rather unusual in having two groups of open fields; an East and West Field for the hamlet of Tebworth, with West Field abutting upon Watling Street, and a similar named pair that served Chalgrave but were in fact located closer to the parish's other hamlet at Wingfield. Part of the medieval fields can still be seen in the landscape in relic ridge and furrow, particularly on the north-east side of Tebworth where the former East Field lay, and the two hamlets are still the more important settlements of the parish. This situation was evidently ancient for in 1376 a rental listed thirty-two messauges at Tebworth and seventeen at Wingfield but only eight around the manor house. The details of the rolls make it clear that the open fields were being operated on a system of strict equality of holdings, for of the fifty-three tenants recorded as holding land in the common fields only one held a virgate of land and all the rest had a half-virgate—about fifteen acres. The strict control of the manorial system appears at its peak, for the down-turn in economic activity that was to dominate the fourteenth century had not yet arrived, bringing with it a breakdown of the close relationships that the villein shared with the soil of his manor. Even so, it is noticeable how many references there are to fines imposed in the manorial court upon those who were already attempting to consolidate their narrow strips into more sensible blocks through voluntary exchange and without the lord's permission.

[13] 'Chalgrave Court Roll, 1278–1313', *Bedfordshire Historical Record Society*, XXVIII (1948).

Another fine group of manorial rolls has been translated for Elton, a substantial village on the north-western border of Huntingdonshire with Northamptonshire, where the annual accounts have survived for the end of the thirteenth century until shortly after the Black Death over seventy years later.[14] The manor was held by the Abbot of Ramsey and it is interesting to see that he was keen to exact the full work services and other dues, particularly in the earlier part of the period. Can it be that Elton had reached the limit of its clearance and cultivation of waste and that the Abbot could see the prospect of rents and dues no longer rising, as they must have surely done in the previous centuries, and was he therefore determined to ensure that the existing dues were maintained?

Elton still has clear traces around it of former arable cultivation of great open fields in the abundant evidence of ridge-and-furrow. Such features are best preserved where farming has gone over to pasture and stock rearing in this century, but even where intensive deep ploughing has taken place aerial photographs can still reveal large areas of medieval open fields. Open field farming dominated the medieval landscape of the two counties. Huntingdonshire contains the best landscape evidence of the two, particularly in the west, but good examples can also be seen around many of the more remote villages in north-west Bedfordshire as well. This lost landscape of the Middle Ages is picked out most clearly in the winter when the low angle of sunlight produces long shadows or allows the morning frost to lie in the hollows of the furrows all day.

Deer parks

Even by the end of the Middle Ages not all of the wasteland had been cleared. At Brampton, it was more valuable to preserve woodland as a source of timber than to reclaim it

[14] Ratcliff, S. C. (Ed.), *Elton Manorial Records: 1279–1352* (1946).

for cultivation. Elsewhere tracts of woodland survived as private deer parks for it was not only the kings of England who had a love for the chase. Many of these parks were owned by the greater magnates, but some deer parks were established by men who had risen to a limited position from complete obscurity, substantial freeholders who had managed to acquire a small but nevertheless official post.

Christopher Saxton's maps, drawn in the late sixteenth century, are one means of identifying these parks, although those that he portrayed are not necessarily of great antiquity. Many of the new deer parks can also be traced because they needed the permission of the Crown for their establishment, but the licences that were granted do not always help to trace their bounds in the landscape today. Saxton shows a concentration of parks around Ampthill and along the Lower Greensand in Bedfordshire while Speed's rather later map of 1610 marks several across mid-Huntingdonshire, but both these areas have suffered much in recent years from field enlargement and the removal of field boundaries so that it is not possible to trace the great earthen banks and ditches that surrounded them. In many cases only the place-name of 'Park' survives in a farm name or it has been left on the Ordnance Survey map as a topographic name. Around Ampthill there are several Park Farms: Littlepark Farm near Ampthill railway station; Park Farm in the south of Steppingley parish; Houghtonpark Farm adjacent to the ruins of Houghton House; Brogborough Park Farm and Beckeringspark Manor Farm. In each case it is difficult to recognise the boundary of the park in the landscape. The same is true of another group of parks that were largely the result of the de Pabenhams being given leave in 1312 to enclose their woods in Carlton and Harrold. There was already a park at Carlton in 1278 for it was said to include a wooded close of twenty acres. The manor to which it belonged was known as *Carlton alias Pabenhams* to avoid confusion with another Carlton Manor. The one manorial home to survive in the present landscape is Carlton Hall which occupies an isolated position in the south-west of the parish. South-west of the house the minor road to Turvey makes a broad curve along the parish boundary—which is continued eastwards on a green lane to Northey Farm—and it would be tempting to recognise part of the park boundary here.

We know rather more about the park that was established in Eaton Bray in the thirteenth century. In 1221 William de Cantlowe had built a house there; in 1273 it was described as having a wall and a moat around it with a drawbridge that allowed access to the deer park. The moated site can still be clearly recognised at Park Farm (Plate 7) and the park boundary lay along the western boundary of the parish, adjacent to Edlesborough in Buckinghamshire, where a curving line can be followed along an over-deepened ditch that runs north to join the River Ouzel. The deer park at Stevington also had a boundary along the edge of its parish. The medieval park covered 140 acres and is recalled today in Park Road, Park Cottage and Park End. The park lay north of the road to Bromham and ran down to the River Ouse five hundred yards away. On its eastern side the boundary can be followed by the curve of the road and the parish boundary, the latter continuing down to the river when the road branches off. Such has been the amount of hedgerow removal in this area that nothing remains of the bank that would have been necessary to keep the deer within the park. However, at Keysoe, because it is partially concealed in woodland the park retains some of its bank. The documentary details of the park are obscure for the manorial records do not mention a deer park, yet Keysoe Park Farm and Keysoepark Wood are clear enough·in the landscape today. The farm is a fine example of a seventeenth-century brick building, but what is more interesting is that it lies just outside the perimeter of a massive semi-circular moat, undoubtedly the site of the farm that had owned the park. There is evidence to the south and east of the farmhouse of medieval ridge-and-furrow so the park cannot have extended in that direction. But if the road to Riseley is followed until it leaves the parish, the area of the park can be recognised in this direction. Here the edge of Keysoepark Wood is marked by a deep ditch and inner bank as a clear reminder of its former purpose.

Clerics as well as laymen had their parks in the Middle Ages. Sometimes the purpose is not always clear, for the monks of Old Warden had Park Grange which is recalled by the name Park Wood in the west of the parish today, together with a farm of the same name. Little Park, Buckden, is unlikely to have been a hunting park for the bishops of Lincoln because of its very small size. It survives today as the grounds of the former bishop's palace, still with the fishponds and the double row of trees along the outer bank that were mentioned in a survey of 1647. The bishops also had Great Park and this was stocked with deer. It is on record that in 1227 permission was given for deer leaps and at a later time over two hundred deer and a keeper's house are mentioned. In 1330 Great Park had been extended by two hundred acres so it was certainly large; only Park Farm recalls its existence today. Buckden is completely devoid of woodland today, but in the great survey of 1086 woodland was a league in length and breadth, most of it probably on the west of the parish, south of the Great Park that was soon to be developed. The farm of Buckden Wood alone bears witness to this vanished element of the landscape.

At Somersham the bishops of Ely had a palace, of which little survives apart from two huge fishponds and some medieval masonry of the stone bridge that once crossed the outer moat. But to the south and stretching onto a great area of common land was a deer park of which the topographic name remains on modern maps. It was the core of a huge hunting preserve in the sixteenth century. From 200 acres in the thirteenth century it was said to be ten miles in circuit three hundred years later. The Somersham Chace, as it became known, still covered 621 acres in 1653. When the Crown had acquired the manor in the early seventeenth century James I proposed restocking the park with deer and using the dilapidated house, which had earlier been used to house captured recusants, as a royal hunting box. Although he appointed a game-keeper it is doubtful if hunting resumed; in 1762 the chace was destroyed by enclosure.

Castle, town, village and farm in the landscape

Hunting in the forests and deer parks was the privilege of the new Norman lords and their descendants. For the peasantry of England the Norman Conquest can have meant little more than a change in the name of their lord, although others undoubtedly suffered hardship and privation. But for the English thanes it was a time of dispossession as the Conqueror carried out the largest redistribution of land that the country has ever witnessed. Many estates were reorganised into large new groups under the control of a powerful Norman lord and it was not at all unusual for such men to hold land over several counties. Nigel d'Albini's new Bedfordshire barony had displaced twenty-five Saxon thanes. The pre-Conquest Church held on to its land with varying degrees of success but with the establishment of a great many new monasteries in the twelfth century their overall share of the land market saw a steady rise.

The new lords felt an immediate need to defend their gains, for England shortly after the Conquest must have remained suspicious and hostile towards its new masters. It was in William I's interest to establish strong defensive works at strategic sites, or where population was centred, from which his appointed sheriffs might maintain a watchful eye. Hence the castle building at Bedford and Huntingdon is hardly surprising for both had been important Saxon settlements and had already been fortified. Bedford was established as a Saxon *burh* by Edward the Elder in A.D. 915, as part of his strategy against the Danish army. It is probable that an important town, with an extensive suburb, had grown up there. Around the suburb was thrown a semi-circular ditch, the King's Ditch, which was to remain a significant feature of the town's morphology until the beginning of the nineteenth century. Practically all of it is lost beneath the streets and buildings of the county town, but on St Mary's Embankment, beside the Bedford College of Higher Education, a short piece of the ditch has been 'preserved'. The new castle of the late eleventh century covered a far smaller area than the King's Ditch. It was confined to the north of the river. The Norman motte and bailey did, however, encroach upon the Saxon town and a number of buildings were demolished, although excavation within the bailey area has so far failed to reveal any trace of the former streets. Part of the curving line of the bailey may be traced along Castle Lane but otherwise only the earthen mound of the motte remains as a visible feature of Bedford's townscape.

It seems likely that the new fortification at Huntingdon was placed partly over the old defences and it is certain that some of the town was demolished for Domesday Book records that twenty houses were removed and a residence of the Bishop of Lincoln displaced. The Norman motte and bailey guarded the important crossing of the Ouse, a place where it is believed that there had been a bridge since Roman times. Part of the earthen motte remains, but the bailey has been greatly mauled by the railway which was driven through it in the nineteenth century. Again in recent years the new by-pass has nibbled away at the edges. Both the railway and road-making have damaged earthworks on Mill Common which lies to the west of the bailey and probably holds the key to the Saxon fortifications of the town.

Elsewhere in the two counties it was the new overlords who were to build for themselves substantial castles, some so large that they were to rival both Bedford and Hunting-don. It is unfortunate that surface remains of the buildings are nowhere to be found; mostly all that remains is a rather subdued system of earthen ramparts. Yielden and Cainhoe are the most impressive among the castle remains, although the view of the latter is ruined from one direction by an untidy rural junkyard. Cainhoe has a most prominent motte, and so it should, for it was the centre of one of the most powerful baronies in Bedfordshire, the d'Albini family who reigned there from the Norman Conquest until the middle of the thirteenth century (see Plates 8 and 9). In 1233 the male line of the family had been extinguished and in 1272 the inheritance was shared by three sisters. Isabella received the 'hall' of Cainhoe and the description that survives shows that the fortress was still in use. But by 1374 it was described as ruinous and only two years later two men were accused of taking away 'freston', timber and tiles from the gate-house and other buildings.[15]

Another powerful barony was centred on Eaton Socon in the eastern side of the county of Bedford, where Eudo Dapifer, the king's steward, built himself a large castle. Unlike Cainhoe the castle had a strikingly important position for it controlled a strategic crossing of the Ouse. Today the crossing is now almost a mile further north. The castle is unfortunately on private land and is much hidden by trees, but aerial photographs have revealed that it had two baileys rather than the normal one. The explanation for this unusual plan seems to lie in the transfer of the castle to the Beau-champs in the early twelfth century—they already had con-trol over Bedford—and the rebuilding that followed. Ex-cavations in the northern bailey have found some forty late Saxon burials, together with evidence for a church and other buildings of that period. Nearby, two other substantial buildings have been located, all pointing to the expansion

---

[15] B.R.O. CRT 130/5 and a note on the castle in *The Bedfordshire Magazine,* X (1965–67), pp. 85–87.

of the castle over part of an older pre-Norman settlement at Eaton Socon.

By the close of the thirteenth century several other castles had been built in Bedfordshire, notably at Thurleigh, Bletsoe, Luton, Odell, Meppershall and Totternhoe, and smaller mounds in a number of places, such as at Mount Hill, Flitwick, suggest other minor fortifications. In Huntingdonshire the list is less impressive for, apart from Huntingdon, mottes appear to have been erected at Kimbolton and Church End, Wood Walton, but elsewhere the landscape is remarkable for its absence of medieval fortifications. Kimbolton Castle today is no longer a defensive work but a graceful house remodelled by Vanbrugh. A small motte in the west of the landscaped park probably marks the site of the medieval castle built in the late twelfth century by Geoffrey FitzPiers, although there may have been an even earlier fortification during the period of anarchy in Stephen's reign. Thomas Stirrup's map of 1673, the earliest map of the estate that has survived, marks 'Castle Hill' behind the formal gardens of the house.[16] It is worth noting at this point that Conington Castle, in the north of the county, is nothing more than the title of a fine seventeenth-century house—unfortunately now demolished—which had itself been the eventual successor to Bruce's Castle. That too had not been a motte and bailey castle but a large moated site. On the other hand the fortification at Church End, Wood Walton is genuine enough. Even so little is known about it. It is generally believed to be a temporary siege castle erected in the troubled times of Stephen and Matilda. In 1134 the manor of Wood Walton had been given to the Abbot of Ramsey and there is no mention of a castle at that time. Then in 1143 Geoffrey de Mandeville, Earl of Essex, occupied Ramsey with soldiers with the intention of fortifying the town against Stephen. He also took the Wood Walton manor and probably began the construction of the motte at

[16] H.R.O. SM 13/63.

Church End as a forward defence line. In the following year Geoffrey de Mandeville died and it was left to his son, Ernold, to complete the work. It is known that he withdrew his soldiers from Ramsey to Wood Walton. After that Wood Walton and the castle at Church End disappear from the record of history; it is unlikely that the motte was ever occupied permanently from that date.

Another of the 'temporary' castles that was to be transformed into a permanent home for a long period was Meppershall. In 1137 William de Meppershall was no doubt grateful for the protection of his new castle after he had declared himself against Stephen and was subsequently besieged. The siege must have proved unsuccessful for the Meppershalls remained in control of the manor until 1493. The attractive timber-framed manor house that lies just south of the church was built by their successors, probably at the beginning of the seventeenth century, but it is within the earthworks of the earlier castle. The motte can just be made out in the trees to the south. The house itself is of great interest for its blackened timbers and wide box-frame is far more familiar in western England than it is in the rest of Bedfordshire.

One wonders why there are fewer castles in Huntingdonshire. Admittedly the county is the smaller of the two and might therefore be expected to support fewer baronies but the answer is more likely to be found in the soil. The cold clays of the upland parishes were unattractive to the great lay landowners and few large estates evolved here in the Middle Ages. A higher proportion of land was held by various ecclesiastical authorities and although they were not above erecting defences to safeguard their property it is likely that such ownership was a restraining influence.

Most of the castles, at least the larger ones, can still be seen in the landscape, but of Luton's there is practically no trace. In 1217 a foreign mercenary, Fawkes de Breauté had found favour with the Crown and was made Sheriff of

Bedfordshire and Buckinghamshire. By all accounts he was an unscrupulous man who was to create many enemies from the way that he seized property and mistreated those who complained of his conduct. In 1221 he had acquired the manor at Luton and immediately set about building a castle there, evicting the occupants of twenty houses in the process of alienating 150 acres for the motte and bailey. He then dammed the River Lea and this caused water to flood the land of the Abbot of St Albans and to render his mill useless. The Abbot's protests were met with abuse, just as the monks of Old Warden had been treated—only rather more severely in their case—when de Breauté had seized some of their land. But the mercenary went too far when he arrested one of the King's justices at the Dunstable Assizes who had given judgement against him, and the young king, Henry IV, was forced to take arms against him. Bedford Castle was besieged and the principal defendants, who included de Breauté's brother, were hanged at the end of the siege. De Breauté had conveniently slipped away and was able to escape the punishment of the others. But Henry ordered that the castle should be slighted and the trenches filled. Some of the stone from Bedford Castle was given to the local priories at Newnham and Caldwell. The castle at Luton must have disappeared at this time and only Castle Street now commemorates it (although it does not lie near the site). The line of the bailey encompassed an area between the parish church, Luton College and the recently constructed inner ring road, with a north-eastern boundary along the River Lea. The river goes through the town in a culvert but emerges for a short distance where the bailey must have run alongside.

One peculiar fortification in Huntingdonshire provides one of the many puzzles that the local historian constantly encounters in his field-work. This is the five-sided moated mound that can be found in the remote west of Conington. Conington Round Hill, as it is known, is now partly obscured by a copse but its origin is even more difficult to trace. Was it an abortive attempt by the Cotton family to build a new manor house, as Professor Pevsner suggests in his encyclopaedic series on The Buildings of England? The Cottons did not acquire the Manor of Conington until the middle of the fifteenth century and it is rather difficult to understand why they should try to build a new house in such an isolated position or to use a defensive style that had been abandoned for at least two centuries. A map of the manor in 1595[17] reveals Bruce's Castle as the 'old scite' with a new manor house some distance to the north, neither of them near the Round Hill. The moat at Bruce's Castle was the site of the court of the manor described in 1279 where a house had probably been built soon after Bernard de Brus had acquired the manor in 1242. It appears to have been in occupation until 1576, presumably by the Cottons since 1460. But we cannot be certain that it was the site where Camden recognised traces of an 'ancient castle' in 1586 or whether that great Elizabethan topographer was referring to Round Hill. Coffin Close is marked on the Conington Tithe Map of 1842 just to the south-west of the mound, and 'Deer Park' is shown to the east, so the site was apparently important at some time. There was only one manor recorded in Domesday Book, but by the thirteenth century the Bevill family—substantial freeholders elsewhere in the county, and after whom Bevills Wood is named—were land-holders in the parish and the defensive mound might be their handi-work. Or was it another of the temporary siege castles of the early twelfth century, for Ramsey lies only a few miles away across the open fen and the castle at Wood Walton is even nearer?

The great landowners were also responsible for the estab-lishment of new towns on their estates. With the culmination of a long period of expansion in the thirteenth century trade saw a natural increase and market centres were booming. At the same time, landlords were beginning to suffer a

[17] V.C.H., Vol. III, p. 144 (1936).

decline in the steady growth of rents and services they had enjoyed for so long, an increase that had resulted from the expansion of agricultural land and production. What better way to increase one's revenue than to establish a new market centre and to tap some of the trade that had developed from a prosperous countryside. Often the new market, with its burgage plots laid out around a market place in order to attract merchants and tradesmen, could be conveniently sited on a part of the manor that had produced little return as agricultural land.

There were few markets in the two counties in the eleventh century. In Bedfordshire the Domesday survey only recorded them on the royal manors of Luton and Leighton and for the small centre of Arlesley. The latter still has an open space in front of the church which probably marks the site of the early medieval market place, and the market place at Leighton Buzzard is a focal point to the existing town. Bedford is not specifically mentioned as the site of a market, but it almost certainly had one for it seems doubtful that the chief Saxon town should have lacked this most important element in the life of an urban community. In Huntingdonshire only Huntingdon itself is certain to have had an early market but the details make up for their absence elsewhere. Two hundred and fifty-six burgesses were living in the four 'quarters' of the town and two of the quarters had eighty residences which belonged to one hundred and forty of them. Yet the town had once been more prosperous for after the Conquest over a hundred plots were said to lie vacant and this was quite apart from the land that had been laid waste as a result of the building of the castle motte and bailey.

By the early years of the fourteenth century the small number of markets was considerably augmented. In Bedfordshire there were fifteen new markets and Huntingdonshire had acquired another five. In most cases the market places that were laid out can still be recognised in the morphology of the settlements and in towns such as St Ives, St Neots and Kimbolton they are the dominant features of the townscape. At Ramsey, however, the wide street of Great Whyte should not be confused with the site of the medieval market place, for that lay at the gate of the abbey and followed the line of the High Street and Little Whyte, at right angles to Great Whyte. The open market place has been encroached upon to such an extent that it is no longer recognisable. Great Whyte can be explained by the existence of a stream which formerly flowed down the centre, the buildings on either side being associated with the water-borne traffic that came in from the larger fenland rivers and reached the town along High Lode. The street appears to have become built up in the seventeenth and eighteenth centuries, but it is probable that the waterway was in use during the medieval period importing stone for the construction of the abbey church and other monastic buildings. Not until the last century was the stream culverted and the street given its present broad appearance.

The newly founded markets appear to have been successful during the Middle Ages, although the location and ultimate fate of the markets at Sundon, Old Warden, Aspley, Silsoe and Blunham remain obscure. These are only small villages today and there is no clear trace in their morphology of a former trading activity; such places are likely to have benefited from the optimism and good fortune that accompanied most of the early medieval creations. Doubtless they succumbed to the economic changes which affected the countryside in the fourteenth and fifteenth centuries. The most successful markets were those that were either established early or sheltered under the protection of one of the greater magnates. At Kimbolton, for example, the castle of Geoffrey FitzPiers appears to have encouraged the foundation of a market, for a charter had been obtained by A.D. 1200. There is mention of burgesses in the town by 1279. The early medieval castle did not overshadow the market place in the way that the present house does, with its gates at the eastern end, but it clearly offered protection. Kimbolton's rectangular market place was laid out in such a manner as to divert the main road, the present A45, through its length thereby gaining from the trade which was forced to pass through and from the tolls which could be levied. The road still makes a sharp right-angled bend at either end of the market place and its earlier alignment can probably be recognised along East Street—a back lane to the market. The long narrow plots of the burgess properties are still faithfully preserved in the building lines that extend back from the market across the former gardens (see Plate 10). To the north of the town, across the River Kym, lies the area still known as New Town although there is little evidence of an urban status today. New Town was one of Kimbolton's medieval settlements and it appears to have been an attempt to expand the market town; in the area today the hedgerows of the fields reveal a series of narrow plots which suggest an abortive attempt at a planned settlement. This might well be one of the many over-ambitious projects whose relics still mark the face of England. On the other hand, New Town was probably planned after the peak of trading activity had been reached at Kimbolton. Like some other new towns of the late Middle Ages, it was doomed to failure.

Although the protection of a castle, or perhaps just a fortified manor house as at Somersham, was a reasonable guarantee against failure, it was those markets that were able to benefit from both road and water-borne traffic that enjoyed the best prospects. The majority of the medieval market towns that we can enjoy today were established at bridgeheads. Two of the most successful were also monastic foundations, St Neots and St Ives both occupying valuable sites alongside the River Ouse. In 1117 St Neots had been separated from its mother parish of Eynesbury when land was granted for the establishment of a Benedictine priory. Close to the important manors of Eynesbury and Eaton and adjacent to the river the monks do not appear to have lost much time or opportunity for by 1180 there was a bridge across the river and traffic was already being channelled through the market place which had been laid out in front of the priory gate. The latter is no longer a visible part of the town's morphology but it lay to the north of the present huge rectangular market place.

At St Ives the markets and the great annual fair were to bring immense prosperity to the medieval town. St Ives' fair held a prime position amongst the annual fairs of eastern England. Merchants came here from great distances, including countries on the further shore of the North Sea. The town had a distinct advantage in its location well downstream from the other markets of Bedfordshire and Huntingdonshire for it was more easily reached by water and could benefit from the traffic of the fenland rivers. The hamlet of Slepe was in existence before the market town was laid out by the monks, for it was recorded under that name in Domesday Book and the church for Slepe, now St Ives parish church, lies at the western edge of the town almost on the river bank. In 974 an estate at Slepe had been given to the monks of Ramsey Abbey and it appears to have been of little significance until 1001 when the bones of St Ivo were reputed to have been found there. We know practically nothing about St Ivo apart from the fact that he was apparently a bishop of Persian origin who had died at Slepe *circa* A.D. 600. Nevertheless, his subsequent canonisation led to the establishment of a priory on the site of the discovery and the renaming of the settlement. The hamlet soon became the centre for pilgrimages and this gave the impetus for a market. In the early twelfth century a charter was also obtained for a fair and some decades later it appears that both market and fair had acquired permanent sites and were being enclosed with buildings. Shortly before the establishment of the twelfth-century fair a bridge had been built across the Ouse. Its successor, the graceful fifteenth-century bridge that is still in use, stands on the line of the first one. The bridge debouched into the very centre of the market town whose market place and fair occupied the long narrow space that has survived into the twentieth century without encroachment (Plate 11). By 1279, the Abbot had seventy customary tenants in the 'Street' (now the Broadway and Market Hill). As at Kimbolton, the long narrow town plots of the market traders can still be recognised clearly in the morphology of the town. What is unusual, however, is the number of narrow alleys and lanes that run at right angles to the market place, on either side of the bridge, and which have the unusual name of 'Wait'. The meaning is obscure but there appears to be a relationship to the Great and Little Whyte of Ramsey, perhaps a local name for the narrow streets whereby river traders had access to the market.

Another town to benefit from a riverside location was Biggleswade, alongside the River Ivel in Bedfordshire. The town developed from a prebendal manor, one of the properties of Lincoln cathedral. By 1227 a market charter had been obtained and a large market place laid out. The burgesses attracted to the new market were not only to receive plots around the market place but had rights of common on the area of common grazing land that was situated to the north of the town. In several of the new towns these grazing rights were jealously guarded by the burgesses and it is one of the reasons for their survival today. At St Neots, for example, Islands Common remains to the north of the town, alongside the River Ouse, still in its unenclosed state.

Other new towns benefited from their location adjacent to a busy road. Among these Dunstable is the most outstanding. It is the only urban community in medieval Bedfordshire and Huntingdonshire to owe its origin entirely to the Crown. In the early twelfth century Henry I carved out a small piece of his estate at Houghton Regis in order to establish a market. The 450 acres of rough ground lay at the junction of the Icknield Way—the prehistoric trackway that one suspects was still used for communications in the Middle Ages—and Watling Street. Local tradition attributes the establishment of Dunstable to the fact that the area was noted for a band of robbers led by a felon named Dun whose thieving activities would be curtailed by a settlement in the area. It is much more likely that Henry saw the possibilities of gain from a market that lay at the crossroad of two important routes. The new market certainly flourished, but the Crown was not to enjoy the fruits of Dunstable's success. In 1132 the new market was granted to an Augustinian priory that had been established there and Dunstable grew through the medieval period under their jurisdiction. The strict control of commercial activities was disliked by the traders and this led to a long history of strife between monk and trader. On one occasion the burgesses were so enraged that they proposed moving their activities to nearby Eaton Bray. The influence of the Crown was not entirely lost, however, for successive English kings had an affection for the town and some of them spent Christmas there. The Old Palace Lodge Hotel recalls the site of Kingsbury, the royal lodge. Henry VIII even chose Dunstable as the place where Archbishop Cranmer should settle the problems of his divorce!

Dunstable displays well many of the characteristics of a new town created from an existing parish. The small size of its administrative area meant that the burgesses could have had no interest in agriculture, although a patch of common grazing was set aside for those in the community who needed animals to carry their goods. Some of the medieval new towns were not allowed a church of their own; their burgesses had to resort to the mother church in the parish from which they had been established. At Dunstable the townspeople were allowed to use the nave of the priory church and this alone accounts for the survival of a twelfth-century monastic church after the Reformation.

The new towns could never have succeeded without the produce from a well-settled countryside or the demand for craftsmen and their products which could be the result only of agricultural communities becoming more specialised and less reliant upon their own resources. The number of new markets that sprang up in the thirteenth century also testifies to the abundance of migrant labour that was available in the rural hinterland of the new towns. The poll taxes and lay subsidies of the thirteenth and fourteenth centuries show that many of the townspeople had names which can be traced from nearby villages. This all implies a countryside that was producing at a maximum, where land was cultivated right up to, and in some cases beyond, the margins of tolerance for medieval cultivation. Bedfordshire and Huntingdonshire were certainly well populated even by the time of the Norman Conquest—a fact that is evident in the pages of Domesday Book. We can be quite sure that the majority of parish boundaries had been determined by then. The new fields that had been carved from the remnants of woodland were not always easily accessible from existing villages. Consequently a large number of small hamlets and lonely farms came into being, often connected by narrow, twisting roads that duplicate themselves in their connection with the larger centres. The parishes of western Bedfordshire contain the best examples of this pattern of roads and dispersed settlement, although this type of landscape can also be recognised on the clay lands north of the River Ouse.

The documentary evidence for the hamlets and farms—secondary settlement—in the late cleared woodland is often lacking. Frequently where clearances from the wood are mentioned there is no mention of any settlement. This does not mean that such settlements did not exist for the documents in question were more concerned with describing those elements of the newly cleared landscape that entailed a change in revenue for the manor. The same argument applies to Domesday Book for that survey was not interested in the disposition of settlements but of the make-up and financial value of the manor. Some occasional references to hamlets occur in the great Norman survey but a far larger number must have been accounted for in a form that is not immediately recognisable. For instance, the three parishes of Gidding—Great, Little and Steeple—were all grouped together under the single name. Only through working out the later manorial histories of the three places and tracing them back to some of the six entries that Gidding received in Domesday Book can we decide whether one of several settlements were recorded. In this case it appears that all three Giddings were probably in existence in the eleventh century. Nearby, at Catworth, we are left in no doubt about Little Catworth for it received separate mention in the survey as Catworth Parva, but as one of the berewicks of Spaldwick.

A number of the hamlets have the familiar place-name ending of End or Green; many of them can be found in early medieval documents. Although the first recorded date of the name may not be significant in all cases for the foundation of the settlement, there is a concentration of dates to be noted around the twelfth and thirteenth century. Sometimes End and Green do not appear as part of the name until several centuries later. Such is the example of Acden Green in Great Staughton which was simply Accadena in 1124; it did not appear as Agden Grene until 1553. Thrup End, Lidlington, was recorded as Trop in 1276 and did not become Thruppe End until 1637. It would seem that not all the early medieval hamlets were as explicitly named as we see them today. Others received their End or Green appellation from an early stage of their history; Wood End, Cranfield was already Wodende in 1250 and Woodmer End, Shillington, was Wodemenende by 1255. These two names clearly relate to a small community that had been newly established on the edge of the remaining waste and there are many others that give us a glimpse into the early medieval environment in this way. Another of Cranfield's hamlets,

Whorley End, was simply Horle in 1244—the dirty or untidy clearing—while Grove Farm was Brechegrove in 1294—land broken up by the plough. Not all of these names can be directly related to new settlement and there may be a few cases where the name simply refers to an area of new land taken in for agriculture and where no settlement appeared until several centuries later. But Leycourt, in a remote corner of Great Gransden, is explicit enough for when it was recorded in 1227 it was referring to 'cottages by the clearing'. Not all of these secondary place-names related to arable agriculture either for there are a number of Herdwick or Hardwick names to be found which tell of a pastoral farm, often one that was involved in sheep rearing. A well-documented Hardwick is found in Gransden parish and first recorded in 1227. Hardwick End, Keysoe, is perhaps even more rewarding for the site is now deserted—close to Keysoepark Wood and Keysoe Park Farm—and the ground is full of the tell-tale humps and depressions of the former house plots.

The isolated farmhouses are even more interesting because the medieval names often contain the name of a freeholder, or that of a manorial lord. We cannot be certain that these names commemorate the pioneers who carved new farms out of the woodland, but it would seem likely that many of them belong to the first farmers. A large number enjoyed manorial status although this was not something that necessarily denoted any position of wealth or influence. Sometimes manorial status appears to have been acquired after the farm had been established, although we are left in the dark as to how the change had occurred. Others resulted from manorial subdivision since Domesday times. A. C. Jones has estimated that there were between three and four hundred manors in Bedfordshire by 1500, an average of three per parish. Single manor parishes were rare whereas they had been the norm at the time of the Domesday survey. Most manors were small; the median size was only some

2250 acres.[18] The eleventh-century manor at Bromham, for example, had been divided into three by 1278 when Bromham, Wakes and Brayes Manor were all in existence. There was a fourth, unrelated manor, Bowels (recalled in Bowels Wood today) also in the parish. At Wootton, the Domesday manor had been divided into three parts and one of those parts had been further subdivided into three. Such was the degree of fragmentation of the manor, much of it occurring before 1300. Some of the new manors were established on the outer edge of the cultivated area of the village. It is clear, therefore, that the making of these petty manors was part of the final onslaught on the wilderness.

Many of the isolated farms were surrounded with a water-filled moat. Between one and two hundred still survive in the landscape, although it is clear from work in recent years on moated farmsteads that a far greater number were formerly in existence. Most of the moated sites are not easy to reach today. The majority have been abandoned by their farmhouses and are to be found in tangled copses a long distance from accessible roads. Although there is a general preference for the heavy claylands, there are very few parishes where no moated sites are known. The clays of Huntingdonshire and western Bedfordshire have the highest densities with an average of five or six moats in many parishes. The Lower Greensand, as might be expected, has fewer moats, and yet that area figured prominently in the clearance of woodland in the early medieval period. Evidently there is no easy correlation to be found between those areas where colonisation of the waste was occurring and the density of moated sites. A more valid correlation might be made between the incidence of moats and the claylands where surface water and poor drainage provided sites suitable for the making of moated farmsteads.

[18] Jones, A. C., 'The Customary Land Market in Bedfordshire in the Fifteenth Century', unpublished Ph.D. thesis, University of Southampton (1975).

It is regrettable that hardly any moats have received more than a cursory inspection from archaeologists. But quite a number of moats have produced chance finds of pottery and this has been one means of ascribing an early medieval date for the origin of most of them. Differences seem to exist between moats lying close to village centres and those in far more isolated positions, in terms of date of construction and status. The excavation of sites close to villages has often produced pottery of the pre-Conquest period. At Willington, for example, the so-called 'Danish dock' between the railway and the River Ouse has yielded evidence showing that it was already a moated farmstead during the eleventh century.[19] At Yelling, in east Huntingdonshire, several fragments of moats may be recognised around the church and the village. One moat has produced pottery of the twelfth century and another shows that it was occupied from the tenth century until the fifteenth. The former had a cobbled courtyard and a timber barn. Cobbled courtyards were a common feature of the moated farms. The great complex of moats that lie close to Manor Farm, Southoe, also contained one, the rectangular tiled area being over a hundred feet in length and surrounded by buildings that were roofed with Colly-weston stone tiles that can still be seen in a few places on the Northamptonshire border. Finds of pottery showed a pre-Domesday occupation of the site.

The majority of the moats that lay close to the villages were the sites of manor houses. At Chawston the manor still occupies practically the same site that it did in Domesday times. There the large double moat of the medieval manor can be seen on the western side of the present building. Investigation of the ground within the moats has revealed occupation that predates the Conquest in substantial amounts of late Saxon pottery that has been ascribed to the Stamford potters. Yet only a mile away to the south another moat, this time in an isolated position within Palaceyard

[19] *Medieval Archaeology*, XIX (1975), p. 249.

Wood, has only yielded medieval pottery. Of course, not all of the Domesday manors are to be found close to the village. One clear exception is at Great Staughton where the main Domesday manor had passed into the hands of Adam de Creting by the late thirteenth century. He is reputed to have built the huge moat, with a raised central mound more like a castle motte, a mile to the south-east of the church and village. It is not possible to decide whether de Creting's fortified manor was removed from the village site or whether it lies over an earlier manor.

Some of the more complex moats are located close to the villages, and this third relationship provides further evidence for believing that moats were first constructed by the more important manorial lords and that they were later copied by those who came into possession of the petty manors and other substantial freeholds which characterised the frontier of agriculture on the very edge of the parish in the medieval period. What first induced manorial lords to make moated farmsteads in the closing decades of the eleventh century remains a mystery. F. V. Emery[20] has suggested that a wide range of reasons, many of them practical, might have been responsible although the need for defence would have been uppermost in most of the lords' minds. De Creting's manor at Great Staughton might well have been constructed with a surrounding moat for the purposes of defence and it was said to have successfully withstood a siege in 1624 when there was a dispute over the ownership of the manor. But many of the manors could never have seen the need for an elaborate defensive system and I am inclined to believe that the majority were built to follow a fashion that was being set by the greater magnates from the late Saxon period until the close of the fourteenth century, a fashion that was first taken up by the wealthier manorial lords and eventually copied by the growing num-

[20] Emery, F. V., 'Moated Settlements in England', *Geography,* 47 (1962), pp. 377–88.

ber of substantial freeholders. Indeed, across the two counties a complete gradation of 'defensive' works can be recognised, from the motte and bailey castles through the large moats and banks that appear to encompass some villages—such as at Covington and Keyston—to the large manorial sites and finally down to the isolated moats on the outer edge of the parishes. This following of fashion by petty lords and small landowners is nothing unique to moated sites for as we shall see later the great halls of the rich and powerful were to be repeated time after time in the new houses of the yeoman farmer in the late fifteenth and sixteenth centuries.

SELECT BIBLIOGRAPHY

Beresford, M., *New Towns of the Middle Ages* (1967).
Dunstable Cartulary, *Bedfordshire Historical Record Society*, XIII (1931).
Godber, J., *History of Bedfordshire* (1969).
Raftis, J. A., *The estates of Ramsey Abbey* (1957).
Wadmore, B., *The earthworks of Bedfordshire* (1920).
Wardon Cartulary, *Bedfordshire Historical Record Society*, X (1925–6).
Appropriate parish histories in the V.C.H. for Bedfordshire (Vols. II and III) and Huntingdonshire (Vols. II and III).

lord of the manor required from his tenants. Certainly the Rolls give little indication of pessimism or alarm and the same could be said of the tax levied in 1297. Yet only a few decades later communities were complaining that they could not meet new taxation demands because of the change in their fortunes.

Joyce Godber has traced the history of the manor at Clapham, a few miles upstream from Bedford in one of the most fruitful sites in the county. Yet in 1333-4 none of the lord's services were commuted. It seems that labour was becoming scarce and the manor was clearly experiencing difficulties. By 1342, *The Inquisitiones Nonarum* suggests through its statistical detail an impending economic disaster. Dr Alan Baker has carried out a valuable analysis of this taxation survey for Bedfordshire, and it is evident that rural decline was well under way in that county a decade before the Black Death had arrived. Returns had been made, based upon the previous year of 1341, for a taxation that was to be based upon corn, wool and lambs. These showed that forty-nine places, out of a total of one hundred and eleven, had abandoned some of their land. In several cases the land had been out of use for a number of years. Nearly half of the county was valued at a lower rate than it had been for the taxation of Pope Nicholas IV in 1291 when the same agricultural products had been used as the basis for assessment. In most cases the reason given was that the land was no longer being cultivated although the complaints made, by jurors for each village, must sometimes be treated with caution. The adjacent parishes of Keysoe, Bolnhurst, Pertenhall and Riseley must have been involved in a certain amount of collusion for their complaint was that they were unable to meet the demands of the new tax because they had been over taxed in the past! Yet one must remember that they all lie on the cold clays in north Bedfordshire, a region that was most affected by agricultural decline. Another important area of decline coincides with the Lower Greensand outcrop.

In both the claylands and the Greensand belt colonisation had continued down to the end of the thirteenth century and here most of the more marginal land could be found. Baker also perceived that the majority of the worst afflicted settlements lay on higher ground, which may suggest the effects of a deteriorating climate.[1]

Apart from excessive taxation and the unexplained reason of abandoned land, the villagers gave a number of more explicit reasons for lower production. Several indicated a shortage of labour, a hint that population was no longer on the increase, while others cited a shortage of corn seed—the consequence perhaps of poor harvests—soil exhaustion and various climatic hazards. On the Lower Greensand the dry, infertile soils that had been the scene of so much clearance activity in the previous century were said to be lacking in fertility in a number of places. At Potton the villagers declared 'the land is sandy there in a dry year and little value' and at Segenho (Ridgmont) they said the soil was 'sandy for the greater part and produced nothing except rye'. Over two hundred acres lay untilled at Segenho in 1341. At Houghton Regis the soil was again blamed for the poor production when it was said to be barren and the people were poverty stricken as a result. Altogether some two thousand acres lay uncultivated in Bedfordshire compared with five thousand acres in Cambridgeshire, but the latter's higher total may reflect the greater extent of poor soils, notable among which are the thin soils of the Chalk whose presence is much more widespread than in Bedfordshire. These figures were undoubtedly exaggerated by those who sought to avoid paying the tax or sought to ensure that they were assessed at as low a figure as possible; but the message of decline is clear enough. The claylands and the Lower Greensand had become less prosperous for arable agriculture in the first few decades of the fourteenth century and in

[1] Baker, A. R. H., 'Contracting arable lands in 1341', *Bedfordshire Historical Record Society*, XXXIX (1970), pp. 7–18.

certain localities it is obvious that some settlements were falling on hard times. This pattern of decline is not uniformly present throughout south-east England. While the Bedfordshire manors were complaining of falling production the Huntingdonshire estates of Ramsey abbey were enjoying a return to a level of prosperity that they had not enjoyed for several years. Earlier, the abbey had been active in renting out some of its demesne land, for late thirteenth-century inflation had meant that high rents could be demanded, itself a consequence of higher wages and declining income from the normal activities of the manor.[2] Yet for the Huntingdonshire manors this could have only been a temporary revival and the overall decline was inescapable.

Deserted settlements

The Black Death of 1348–50 must have left deep scars on the social and economic life of most of these impoverished communities. The mortality statistics amongst the greater part of the population in those two dreadful years are unfortunately unavailable to us and those figures that are, most notably those concerning the clergy and monks, invariably provide a biased picture. Priests might well be expected, given the nature of their calling, to be more susceptible to catching the disease; those who lived in closed communities would have had even less chance of escape. In the town of Bedford, for example, all of the clergy were said to have perished apart from the priest of All Hallows, and he only probably escaped by taking the drastic step of resigning. At the priories of Caldwell and Newnham, on the outskirts of the town, both abbots died in the plague years. In Bedfordshire alone the deaths of priests from fifty-four benefices were reported. At Chalgrave, Dunton and Wymington two priests died in quick succession. Over the Lincoln diocese as a whole forty per cent of the benefices became vacant

[2] Raftis, J. A., op. cit.

between Lady Day (March 25) 1349 and Lady Day 1350, facts that hint at the terrible toll exacted by the Plague.

From those manors for which we have details of the plague years a variable picture is gained although the overall impression is of a major disruption of the normal agricultural year. At Caldecote, in north Huntingdonshire, an inquisition post mortem for 1352 shows the manor to be in a bad state. Many houses were said to be ruinous, as was the mill, and the plague was still rife. But the village did not become deserted as a result of the Black Death for although it is now a deserted site collapse did not occur until long after the fourteenth century. Elton shows a similar pattern of temporary dislocation through the plague. There the community had three reeves during the plague year 1349–50 not because of the demise of two of them, it appears, but through the reluctance of villagers to take on the responsible task of organising the day-to-day running of a manor that was plainly experiencing difficulties in reaching its normal production levels and where the collection of rents and dues was often impossible through the death of villeins. John Blakeman, reeve from September 29, 1349, until November 10, 1350, 'prayed' for an allowance of ten shillings of the tallage of the cellarer—the manor was held by the Abbot of Ramsey—for 'divers tenements of bondmen being in the hand of the lord by reason of the mortality which happened in the preceding year'. Twenty-three virgates of land rendered nothing in oats and the rent of eleven cottages was lacking. The lord's customary dues of eggs and honey were not received and the fulling mill was broken and useless and in each case the same reason, the mortality of the previous year, was given. Two years later things werè by no means back to normal for rents were still said to be in decay and the smithy had fallen down, and there was no one prepared to repair it.[3] At Stevington in mid-Bedfordshire the dovecote was in ruins, the fulling mill not working and the

[3] Ratcliff, S. C. (Ed.), *Elton manorial records, 1279–1351* (1946).

produce of the manor garden worth nothing. Here again there was no question of the manor suffering anything more than a temporary reversal in its fortunes, although such a decline might equally have taken a century or more to overcome.

Only at Cainhoe is there some suggestion that the community was unable to recover from the effects of the Black Death. The village was deserted soon after 1350. In 1349 an inquisition post mortem stated that the pestilence had wiped out the bondmen and cottars. Another inquisition, in 1374, was held following the death of the manorial lord, John Dakeney. The Manor of Cainhoe was still said to have some cottages but 'of which ten have newly fallen into the lord's hands owing to the pestilence'. The house, which was presumably the castle, built by Nigel d'Albini at the Norman Conquest, was no longer inhabited and two years later two men were accused of taking away 'freston' (freestone) from the site, together with timber and tiles, some of it from the 'yathouse' (gatehouse). The little twelfth-century chapel that had served the community was also in ruins. By the early sixteenth century it is noticeable that Thomas Rowse was renting the site of Cainhoe Manor, there being no suggestion of any buildings remaining.[4] The site of this small village has remained something of a mystery until recently when aerial photographs have revealed a series of house plots to the east of the castle motte and close up against the bailey (see Plate 9).

The most commonly cited cause of village desertion in the latter half of the Middle Ages is not, however, the Black Death, but the depopulating efforts of landowners seeking to maximise their falling profits through a conversion of the arable to sheep pasture, a process that involved both enclosure of the fields and a scattering of the village population. There is little direct evidence to support such de-

---

[4] Phillips, M., 'Cainhoe Castle', *Bedfordshire Magazine,* X (1965–7), pp. 85–7, and B.R.O. CRT 130/5.

populations to make way for large-scale sheep farming in Bedfordshire and Huntingdonshire. But one must always remember that a lack of documentary evidence may help to explain this view of the desertion of settlements in the two counties. We can be certain that depopulation for sheep pasture was partly a consequence of the falling yields from arable land during the second half of the fourteenth century and throughout most of the fifteenth. It is this aspect of the medieval economy that is more important in the ultimate demise of many of the settlements rather than a deliberate and determined policy of the manorial lord. A. C. Jones has shown how the land market was depressed in Bedfordshire throughout the fifteenth century,[5] a steady decline that was most noticeable on the heavy clays. At the same time there was an increase in peasant mobility and some manorial rent rolls show a steady decline as peasants sought better opportunities elsewhere. In some places the decline continued beyond the end of the Middle Ages and a number of the so-called deserted medieval villages did not in fact become depopulated until the eighteenth and nineteenth centuries. Only at Higham Gobion in Bedfordshire can we be quite certain that depopulation was the direct result of enclosure for sheep pasture during the critical period of the late fifteenth century when so many of the settlements of the east Midlands are now known to have been depopulated. The manorial account rolls of Higham Gobion in 1379–82 show that the village had been seriously affected by the Black Death for the land of John Halewell, John Wilgod, Thomas Neweman, John Smyth, Walter Aleyn and Robert Bonde were all said to have been taken into the lord's hand, presumably because the tenants were no longer living. By 1519 an ecclesiastical visitation described the parish as enclosed and that there was but one parishioner.

A number of Huntingdonshire villages had been deserted by the close of the sixteenth century. At Washingley, where

[5] Jones, A. C., op. cit.

the grass-covered house plots can be recognised close to Washingley Park Farm on the northern side of the minor road that runs between Folksworth and Lutton in Northamptonshire, the Hundred Rolls, compiled in 1279, record forty-two tenants. But by 1332 only twenty-seven were on record. By 1436 the vill was claiming fifty per cent tax relief and twelve years later this had risen to sixty-seven per cent. Church institutions had probably ceased by then for the church was in ruins by 1534. Whether the settlement had been finally destroyed for sheep pasture we cannot tell. The amount of land devoted to sheep was certainly on the increase at that time, but there is no record for the manor itself. The survival of the house plots in the twentieth-century landscape indicates that pasture has been the dominant feature of the site since the village was deserted. Not far from Washingley we come to Little Gidding, where only a farmhouse, now used as a retreat centre, survives together with the exquisite little church that was rebuilt some time after the site had been deserted. It had always been a small place and only ten households were paying tax in the 1428 assessment. The papers of Nicholas Ferrar, among the archives of Magdalene College, Cambridge, give us some insight into the fortunes of the village in the sixteenth century. Ferrar founded a small religious community at Little Gidding in 1625 when he had sought a quiet and secluded place. The manor house was in a dilapidated condition and the church was almost in ruins. The sacristy had been turned into a pig sty and the nave was in use as a barn. Amongst Ferrar's papers there is a note concerning an enquiry made in 1594 into a dispute between the lord of the manor, a Mr Drewell, and the incumbent. The document states that 'twenty years ago the land of Little Gidding was open and has since been enclosed'. If this is a reference to enclosure for sheep pasture, it is certainly a late example of a process that had ceased many decades before elsewhere as a result of the reviving profitability of arable land. Little

Gidding appears to have remained under pasture ever since, although the surrounding open fields have now lost most of their traces of former ridge and furrow as a result of recent ploughing. The house plots together with a moated site can be seen clearly between the main road and the church.

About the same time as the enclosure of Little Gidding Sir Robert Cotton seems to have tried to enclose part of his estate at Conington. A jury report in the early years of the seventeenth century stated that 'about twelve years last past and since [he] hath derayed seven houses of husbandry with the barnes, stables and outhouses'.[6] The 205 acres of arable associated with the houses had been converted to pasture and some forty to fifty persons displaced. Sir Robert's defence was that one house had blown down in a gale while another abutted onto his terrace and gardens. He had also erected new cottages at nearby Denton where some of the tenants had been rehoused. Yet one cannot mistake this for anything but an attempt to reduce the population involved in arable cultivation.

Some desertions in the two counties were the result of enclosure, but not all of them relate to the important period of the second half of the fifteenth century. A. R. H. Baker has suggested[7] that the years between 1552 and 1581 marked a transition between an earlier period of high prices for wool and a later one when rising grain prices made arable more profitable, a period which, on balance, slightly favoured wool and which might therefore account for some of these late desertions. But for the great majority of the deserted villages in Bedfordshire and Huntingdonshire (see Fig. 8) the evidence is far less certain. By the close of the sixteenth century over thirty settlements had been deserted, many of them leaving no surface remains in the present landscape

---

[6] H.R.O. CON5/12/2.

[7] Baker, A. H. R., 'Changes in the Later Middle Ages' in Darby, H. C. (Ed.), *A New Historical Geography of England before 1600* (1976), p. 199.

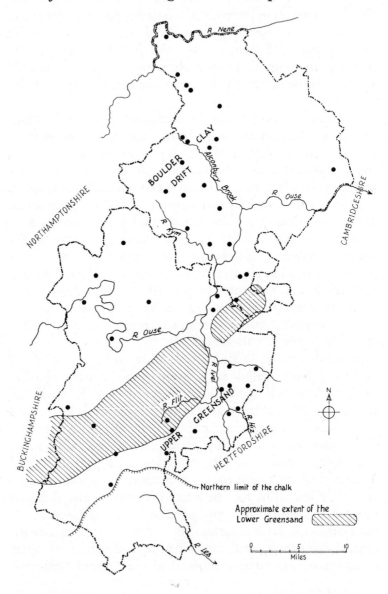

Fig. 8. The late medieval deserted settlements of Bedfordshire and Huntingdonshire.

and there is little firm evidence about them in the documents of the period. Most of the deserted settlements are concentrated on the Greensand in mid-Bedfordshire and the clays of north-west Huntingdonshire. Their distribution reveals the poverty of arable farming in these regions during the fifteenth century. Those that have survived longest as visible objects in the landscape are to be found in Huntingdonshire. In Bedfordshire the gradual conversion of the Greensands to arable has meant the destruction of most of the house plots, tofts and lanes that are the characteristics of medieval deserted villages. Coppingford, Huntingdonshire, lies under permanent pasture and provides one of the most rewarding deserted villages in the two counties. Permission to visit must be obtained beforehand, but there it is possible to locate the site of the moated manor house, the small church that stood close by and the buildings of the village grouped around a small green. Washingley, Little and Steeple Gidding and Little Catworth are all places worth exploring in the same county. The finest example in Bedfordshire is Chellington although not much is known about the date or the reason for its desertion (see Plate 12). The church there still stands—converted into a diocesan youth centre—in a solitary position on a low hill overlooking the River Ouse. Between the church and Hill Farm, which lies several hundred yards to the east, the indistinct mounds of a long straggling settlement can be discerned. In a discontinuous line the deserted village of Chellington can be traced much further east to Freer's Wood; on either side the ridge and furrow of the former open fields is still clearly visible. Chellington Manor disappeared as an individual unit in 1359 when it was combined with Carlton. After that it is no longer recorded separately. Can Chellington be viewed as another casualty of the Black Death?

Elsewhere in Bedfordshire the record of desertion is often to be traced only in a few fragmentary documentary references; the landscape has no story to tell. Until a few years ago the faint surface outlines of the former buildings of Lower Gravenhurst could be recognised in the field, but recent ploughing has made it all but invisible except to the aerial photographer. Air photographs show a number of building plots in the field below the isolated church and stretching behind Rectory Farm. The damaging effect of mechanised farming has also erased a deserted site at Leighton Bromswold in mid-Huntingdonshire. There the field that lies to the south of the church once contained visible evidence of the village having been removed from one site and rebuilt elsewhere; now it is regularly ploughed and looks no different from its neighbours.

Much of the attention of researchers into deserted settlements has been focused upon villages rather than hamlets or individual manor houses. This is understandable when it is recognised that the latter are often so poorly recorded that it is impossible to compile a documentary framework of their evolution through the Middle Ages as a background to a twentieth-century excavation. The work of the Deserted Medieval Village Research Group began by tracing the disappearance of settlements that had been recorded in taxation lists such as Lay Subsidy Returns and Poll Tax Returns. The early lists of deserted sites therefore reflect these medieval sources. But there are many other earthworks, former settlements, that are now known through the use of aerial photographs, archaeological discoveries and local searches through archives that have considerably altered our understanding of deserted medieval villages. For instance, the recognition of several deserted manor houses alone has expanded the total of depopulated sites in the two counties. What is perhaps even more important, however, is the very considerable amount of settlement movement and the shrinkage of villages that has also been identified, primarily from aerial photographs. Until some of these have been excavated, however, we can only guess at when they were abandoned, although it is certain that some of them must have been

Plate 14 The Great Tower at Buckden, formed part of the palace of the fifteenth-century bishops of Lincoln, who also had a large deer park nearby. It is one of the earliest brick structures in eastern England.

Plate 15 The magnificent stone spire of St James' church, Spaldwick, rises over 150 feet and is characteristic of the churches of west and north Huntingdonshire. In front of the church lies the enclosure of Bury Field, where subdued earthworks probably indicate the site of the medieval manor house.

Plate 16 The interior of St Mary's, Haddon. The simplicity of this little church is typical of those to be found on the cold claylands in northern Huntingdonshire. The Norman chancel arch and thirteenth-century chancel reflect the last period of rebuilding to affect the area.

Plate 17 The fifteenth-century gate-house to Tilsworth Manor Farm is one of only two such gate-houses to survive in the two counties. The house is modern and the gate-house now has an eighteenth-century roof, when it was used as a dove-cote.

Plate 18 The ruins of Houghton House near Ampthill. The brick mansion was built in the early years of the seventeenth century and served as the House Beautiful in Bunyan's *Pilgrim's Progress*. In spite of its charm and prominent eminence atop the Lower Greensand scarp it has had an unhappy history and has lain empty for the past two centuries.

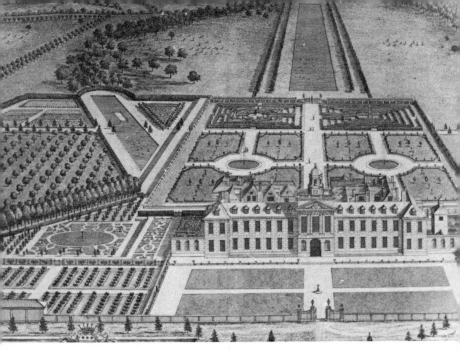

Plate 19 Wrest Park in 1705. Kip's fine engraving shows the formal style of a country park before the great era of landscape gardening. The house had but recently been provided with a new front and the gables of the earlier Tudor façade can still be seen behind.

Plate 20 The print of 1735, below, shows how the park had been substantially altered within thirty years, with the addition of pavilions and other garden 'furniture'. Yet the Grand Canal remained a dominant feature, as it does today.

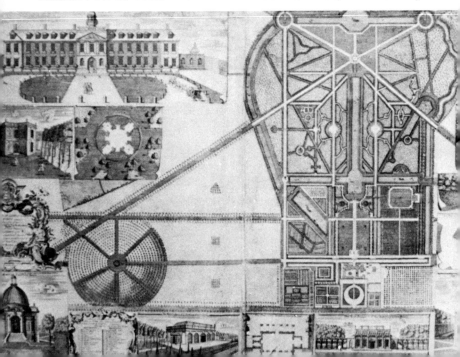

Plate 21 Little Gidding. Earthworks nearby indicate the site of the deserted village and manor house but the exquisite little church remains, its richly furnished interior and college seating style recalling Nicholas Ferrar's little religious community of the seventeenth century.

Plate 22 The classical lines of Eggington House, constructed in the late seventeenth century, pre-date by some years the Georgian façades of town house and country mansion that are to be found elsewhere in the two counties.

Plate 23 An estate worker's cottage at Southill. Upon the acquisition of the Southill Estate in 1795 Samuel Whitbread created a number of new cottages in the village that adjoined the great house and its park, some of them built in a rather elaborate style.

Plate 24 The middle of the nineteenth century marked the peak of the great estates and of their building activity. This group of houses at Ampthill are typical of the rather mundane styles adopted by the Bedford Estate, whose familiar monogram appears on the gable ends of each house.

Plate 25 In sharp contrast are the estate houses of Old Warden, built by Lord Ongley before the Shuttleworths acquired the property with the ornate porches, rustic timber and thatched roofs.

Plate 26 Upton in 1659. This detail from a map of the Manor of Upton reveals the completely open nature of the area in the seventeenth century, with its three great open fields and empty common. Only the windmill stands outside the nucleated village and a fragment of woodland survives in the north-east of the manor.

Plate 27 The Bullock Road at Moonshine Gap, Glatton. The great width recalls its use as a cattle drove road down to the end of the eighteenth century, paralleling the turnpiked Great North Road from Wansford to Alconbury.

attributable to the same general economic decline that seems to lie behind the total desertion of some villages. Over the clays of North Huntingdonshire, for example, there are very few settlements that do not exhibit shrinkage to some degree and the same is true of the adjoining part of north-west Bedfordshire. At Souldrop the small closes around the church show clear signs of former house plots. A few miles to the east, at Keysoe Row, what is now a discontinuous row of houses, some dating back to the seventeenth century, was formerly much more continuous as the earthen mounds that lie in between indicate. These shrunken sites cannot be divorced from their deserted neighbours. Close to Souldrop, but just over the border in Northamptonshire, lies the deserted village of Caldecott and the shrunken site of Newton Bromswold. Both place-names are significant for they indicate marginal settlements established late in the process of colonisation. Caldecott—or cold cottages—is not that unusual as a place-name of a deserted site, not sur-prisingly perhaps, and there are two such places alone in Huntingdonshire where no village survives.

Some of the deserted sites can be recognised today by the survival of the church, as for example, at Caldecote (N. Hunts.), Little Gidding, Chellington, Chalgrave and Lower Gravenhurst. However, the presence of an isolated church does not always denote depopulation. At Bolnhurst and Keysoe, close neighbours in north Bedfordshire, there ap-pears to be no justification for seeking such an explanation. Both parishes consist of scattered hamlets and farms and their churches seem to have been sited to provide easy access to a majority of the members of their dispersed parishes. It has been suggested that there is a former village around the isolated church at Wood Walton, on the edge of the Fens, but so far no positive evidence has been forthcoming to justify this idea. Field-walking, a technique now much prac-tised by archaeologists, has failed to produce any trace of settlement, usually in the form of pottery and building

debris, in the fields around the church. A different explanation must be found for the isolation of the church at Wood
Walton. Was this another place central to a number of
scattered hamlets? Or is the position of the church determined by its foundation on the site of a former heathen
temple in a prominent position on a hill?

Churches eccentric to their present villages have been
identified as survivals of earlier cores of settlement at Biddenham and Little Barford, both alongside the Ouse.
Church End, Biddenham (see Plate 13), has recently acquired a number of new houses with the spread of commuter
homes around Bedford but up till now it has stood aloof
from the village which was grouped around a long, narrow
green. Aerial photographs have shown where an earlier
village lay, between the church and the river, and although
the site is now cultivated the clumps of weeds that concen-
trate on certain parts of the field can still indicate individual
house sites. Field walking here has produced pieces of
medieval pottery and foundation stone. At Little Barford
the village lay around the church and manor house, but the
settlement has since migrated eastwards to re-align itself
along the B1043 road. Finally, at Old Weston, on the
Huntingdonshire clays, field-walking has also identified
traces of settlement around the church, the present village
lying a quarter of a mile to the east.

Many of the deserted sites housed only very small communities. In Huntingdonshire the settlements of Sawtry
Judith, Midloe and Ogerston were little more than the
outlying estates of monasteries, granges that were provided
with a chapel. The church of St Mary at Sawtry Judith had
been part of the endowment when the manor had been given
to the monks of Sawtry Abbey, and it seems likely that it
was soon transferred to the gate-house of the abbey for
documents of the late twelfth century tell of a parochial
church there of that name. Sawtry Judith has been investigated by officers from Monks Wood Experimental Station.

They have identified a manor house, several homesteads and outbuildings as well as roads. The whole settlement was surrounded by a perimeter ditch and bank. Pottery showed that occupation had lasted for some two hundred years from the thirteenth until the fifteenth century. The earthworks of Sawtry Judith are still visible from the road that runs past Whitehall towards Coppingford, but it is interesting to note that Archers Wood has encroached over part of the site since its desertion. Ogerston lay close to the Bullock Road in the west of Washingley parish and only the faint outline of a moat survives to mark the location of a manor of the Knights Templar. Until a few years ago, however, alongside the Billing Brook and a short distance north of the moat, the earthworks of the small hamlet could also be identified in the field. A large circular mound there might well have been the site of a round 'Temple' church.

Several other places are known where small chapels served the community of hamlet and manor farm. At Salome in the parish of Leighton Bromswold only a farm remains to mark the site of a medieval hamlet, but excavations have found rubble and glass of the fourteenth-century chapel that formerly stood there. Priestley Farm at Flitwick in Bedfordshire marks the site of another small hamlet where Nigel d'Albini of Cainhoe Castle had held one and a half hides of land in the eleventh century. The small estate did not acquire manorial status until the fourteenth century but in 1353 Edmund de Bolestrode founded a small chapel there. It is not known when the hamlet at Priestley Farm shrank to its present size, but one suspects that settlement was already reduced by the end of the Middle Ages.

Knowledge and research on deserted sites are undergoing a rapid reappraisal as the result of the new sources of information. The English landscape contains a great variety of depopulated sites, as well as those that survive only in a shrunken state, whose desertion can be attributed to a wide variety of causes and periods. It is almost certainly true that the majority began to experience decline during the second half of the fourteenth century and may well have disappeared before 1500 but we cannot be completely certain without far more investigation of sites, both through documents and on the ground.

A slow recovery

Within a century and a half of the Black Death ten per cent of the settlements of rural England had been erased from the landscape. These changes give a clear sign of an economic decline of considerable magnitude, but there is also some evidence remaining in the landscape that the disaster was often localised and that some communities were beginning to experience a degree of recovery quite early in the fifteenth century. Not all men were despondent and pessimistic and some of the greater landowners were prepared to spend lavishly on new buildings. The fifteenth century brought a revival in eastern England of the use of brick as a building material, an art that had been lost since Roman times. A few buildings in East Anglia had made use of bricks, almost certainly imported from the Low Countries, during the previous two centuries, but it was not until the middle of the fifteenth century that brick-making revived in England. Two early brick buildings survive in Bedfordshire and Huntingdonshire, one at Buckden and the other at Someries Castle, just south of Luton.

Throughout the Middle Ages Buckden was the property of the bishops of Lincoln. Between 1472 and 1480 Bishop Rotherham began building the great brick tower that dominates the centre of the village today, even overawing the spire of the church which stands alongside. It was probably completed by his successor, Bishop Russell, 1480–94. Apart from the tower (see Plate 14) the inner and outer gate-houses, also in brick, and part of the tall curtain wall survive. But of the Great Hall only fragments remain and the rest of the buildings on the site are of nineteenth-century or modern origin. The brickwork is in a fine state of preservation, the deep red bricks, smaller and narrower than present-day bricks and set in the English bond pattern rather than the later universal Flemish bond, are interspersed with diaper patterns of blue, vitrified bricks. The rectangular tower with polygonal turrets on each corner, bears a striking resemblance to that other great brick 'keep' of eastern England at Tattershall in Lincolnshire, built by Ralph, Lord Cromwell, in 1434–5. One wonders whether the bishops of Lincoln copied the design of this palace that was already within their diocese? The style itself is rather retrogressive for a substantial country house of that period, for the greater lords of England had little need for personal defence in the late fifteenth century and houses elsewhere were already beginning to abandon any pretensions they had towards defensive features. Again, Buckden tower cannot have been planned with any serious motives of defence in mind, for the presence of large windows, almost at ground level, and near square corners would have made it an easy target.

Building in brick must have been prohibitively expensive, a luxury few could afford even in the early seventeenth century. Whoever built the brick gate-house at Someries— and there is still much uncertainty about the identity of its founder—must have been one of the wealthiest men in Bedfordshire. The structure stands on the site of an earlier manor house that had been the thirteenth-century home of William de Someries. Unlike Buckden, it is a ruin, rather too close to the runway of Luton Airport to make a visit a pleasure. As yet Someries gate-house is uncared for. The story goes that John Wenlock began the construction of the house, but he fell in the Battle of Tewkesbury in 1471 and it is not known how far the work had then progressed. He was also responsible for the addition of a chapel to the parish church at Luton. The estate of Someries passed to Thomas Rotherham, Bishop of Lincoln and the builder of Buckden tower. It may well be that the bulk of the gate-house is his work for a change can be detected in the pattern of the brickwork a short distance from the ground that appears to indicate the coming of a new builder. There is a small chapel in the gate-house with an exquisite little spiral staircase entirely composed of brick, including a recessed hand-rail. The rest of the house has vanished without trace, but a large moat-like depression lies to the west of the gate-house and the presence of early bricks in the adjacent eighteenth-century cottages suggest that the building was once much extensive and that part of it has served as a quarry for humbler buildings.

Another hint of prosperity in the fifteenth century is contained in the major rebuilding of many of the parish churches in the new Perpendicular style. In Huntingdon-shire a third of the churches were so refashioned in the new style so that the overall impression is of a fifteenth-century church. A similar number—twenty-five—but a smaller por-tion of Bedfordshire churches were so treated. Yet few of these churches were large, far smaller than their counterparts in the thriving textile areas of east Anglia. Several churches were partially reconstructed in the fifteenth century; this normally involved either the tower or the replacement of windows. At Somersham, the lord of the manor, the bishop of Ely, added a new tower, aisle windows and crenellation. But Somersham is still essentially an Early English church. In the intractable claylands of northern Huntingdonshire, where the deserted sites and shrunken villages abound, there are few examples of the new Perpendicular style. Here the majority of the churches were rebuilt in the thirteenth century, before the years of economic change. The shrunken village of Haddon has a church whose interior is still typical of the twelfth century with a simple chancel arch and fine examples of early carving (see Plate 16) while the tower belongs to the thirteenth century. It is clear that these settlements were taking longer to recover than those in more favourable parts of the county. Indeed, only in the towns can one find the finest examples of fifteenth-century rebuilding. The most impressive and exciting church in Bedfordshire was newly built late in the fifteenth century at St Neots, but it is closely rivalled by those of Luton, Leighton Buzzard, Bedford and Biggleswade. In Huntingdonshire, the county of spires, St Ives and Kimbolton churches perhaps lay claim together to the splendour and reviving wealth of the late medieval towns.

One other feature of the late medieval landscape reflects the rising trade of the small market towns and that is the rebuilding of many of the major bridges. For the first time bridges were built in stone and their survival down to the present day is an indication of the skill of their architects and the durability of stone as compared with wood. St Ives and Huntingdon both have surviving examples of narrow fifteenth-century bridges with closely spaced arches and cut-waters on the upstream side to break the force of the water against the piers. Part of the medieval bridge chapel (see Plate 11) still stands at St Ives, one of only three remaining in the country. Old Bedford bridge once had a chapel, but it was destroyed when the whole structure was replaced in 1811–13; early prints reveal again that it was a late medieval building. Elsewhere, the bridges at Harrold, Great Barford and Biggleswade were all either rebuilt or extensively repaired in this period.

It is unfortunate that there is little architecture of the fifteenth century surviving within Bedfordshire and Huntingdonshire to testify to a widespread revival in prosperity (see Plate 17). Neither are there many examples of domestic building from the following century but there is enough to suggest that the Tudor period was a time when an air of optimism returned generally to the rural landscape. This was also to be a time of dramatic changes in landownership and the beginning of the end for the majority of small farmers. Within two centuries of the dissolution of the monasteries most of the land of the two counties had passed into the hands of the great proprietors and the majority of farmers were tenants rather than owner-occupiers. The wind of change that was to sweep across the landscape through the political machinations of Henry VIII brought many new landed families into Bedfordshire—rather fewer to Huntingdonshire—who were to be the founders of the great estates of the eighteenth and nineteenth centuries. Almost a hundred years after Henry had destroyed the monasteries and confiscated their wealth Edmund Gibson, the reviser of Camden's *Britannia,* was to say of Huntingdonshire 'that most of the County being Abby-land, upon the dissolution many new purchasers planted themselves therein'.[8] It is to that process and its consequences that we shall look in the next chapter.

SELECT BIBLIOGRAPHY

Beresford, M. W. and Hurst, J. G., *Deserted Medieval Villages* (1971).
Godber, J., *History of Bedfordshire* (1969).
Hervey, S. H. A., *Two Bedfordshire Subsidy Lists,* 1309 and 1322. *Suffolk Green Books,* No. XVIII (1925).
Leadam, I. S. (Ed.), *The Domesday of Inclosures 1517–18,* Vol. II (1897).
Smith, T. P., 'Someries Castle', *Bedfordshire Archaeological Journal,* III (1966), pp. 35–51.

[8] Camden, W. Britannia. First published in 1595. Gibson's revision, with additional notes, was published in the early seventeenth century. Taken from a facsimile of the same, 1971.

5. The impact of the great estates

New houses and parks. The estate village and farm.

New houses and parks

THE DESERTION OF villages and hamlets and the conversion of arable land to sheep pastures aroused so many
complaints of unnecessary or forced eviction of villagers
that an official inquiry was ordered in 1517, rather too late
for many to seek redress from the courts. That inquiry is
valuable because it provides a picture of landownership in
the early sixteenth century. Bedfordshire it seems was a land
of small freeholders; only a quarter of the land was in the
hands of lay manorial lords. We are not told the proportion
of land that was directly under the control of the monasteries, but it is unlikely to have been as high as for Huntingdonshire where the large abbeys of the fen and fenland edge
had control over large parts of the county. Three centuries
later the pattern of landownership had changed dramatically
and was concentrated in the hands of a few, the church
holding a very small portion indeed. When the government
carried out a survey of landownership in 1873 it revealed
that over half of Bedfordshire was in the hands of less than
fifty persons, and the estates of the Russells, de Grey, St
John, Crawley and Whitbread families encompassed a huge
area in excess of 71,000 acres. In Huntingdonshire, the Earl
of Manchester and the Cotton family held sway over many
farms and villages in the centre and north of the county.
The monasteries whose estates had helped found the fortunes
of the famous landed families were now forgotten ruins or
had already disappeared completely from the landscape.

Following the dissolution most of the religious houses

stood empty and were soon robbed of their valuable facing
stone and stripped of the precious stores of lead in their
roofs. Monastic buildings close to the towns suffered most.
In Bedford the stone of Newnham and Caldwell priories
ended up in houses of the town or in nearby Willington as
part of the house and outbuildings of one of the despoilers,
John Gostwick. Gostwick had been an ordinary yeoman
farmer but gained possession of the manor of Willington as
part of his reward for assisting Henry VIII in the destruction
of the Bedfordshire monasteries. The Tudor dove-cote and
stable of his manor house still survive. At the more isolated
sites, such as the Cistercian houses of Sawtry and Old
Warden, their extinction was less dramatic, though both
sites have little to show today apart from shallow earthworks
that mark the location of old walls (see Plate 5). In recent
years part of Old Warden has been re-excavated and attractive tiled floors that had been left *in situ* by earlier investiga-
tors have been lifted and are now on display at the Bedford
Museum. Rarely the monastic churches survived the dissolution. As a rule only part of the building has been left for
the worship and enjoyment of later generations. This occurred at Elstow and Dunstable, both in Bedfordshire,
where the part of the monastic church that had been used
by the inhabitants of the neighbouring settlement, the nave,
was saved from destruction. At Ramsey the twelfth-century
parish church is not a remnant of the monastic church, for
it stood beyond the abbey gate and was probably the guest
house or *hospitium* of the abbey.

Over the ruins of some of the abbeys rose the great houses
of the new landed gentry. The Gostwicks built for themselves not only the house at Willington but also one at Old
Warden. The Gostwick's house at Old Warden did not
swallow up the whole of the monastic site, but it incorporated part of the abbot's lodging in a new brick gate-house.
Today this is the only part of the mansion to survive;
fortunately it has been restored and provides a good example

of the use of early brick in the county. The rest of the house was demolished at the end of the eighteenth century.

Several other families took the opportunity to build new houses on their recently acquired monastic properties within a few years of the dissolution. Sir Richard Cromwell gained large estates in Huntingdonshire that had formerly belonged to the monks of Ramsey and the nuns of Hinchingbrooke. Without delay he began the building of new mansions on the sites of the two monasteries. Both are now schools, but Hinchingbrooke retains much of its sixteenth-century charm; restoration in the nineteen-sixties revealed that Cromwell had not destroyed the old nunnery completely but had incorporated in his rebuilding a large part of the church and the entrance to the chapter house. The large bay windows are probably an original feature of the new house. Perhaps the most intriguing feature of Hinchingbrooke is the elaborate gate-house, parts of which were transported from Ramsey to be re-erected there. The remainder of the gate still stands at Ramsey, where Cromwell also converted part of the abbey church into his mansion. The nucleus of the present house was probably the Lady Chapel.

Bushmead Priory in north Bedfordshire was the object of a struggle for ownership between the St John family and Sir William Gascoigne. The St John family at Bletsoe were said to be anxious to acquire Bushmead priory because

> it lay so near his (St John's) house that if he should be driven to remove he could find no place so meet . . . but I hear Mr Gasgyne labours for the same.

This comment, made in a letter by Sir Francis Bryan to Cromwell in 1537,[1] concerned Sir William Gascoigne of Cardington who had exchanged land with the King and sought further recompense. In the same year the exchange was confirmed in his favour, but by 1562 the estate of

[1] V.C.H. *Bedfordshire,* Vol III (1912), p. 197.

Bushmead had passed to the de Gery family from Cambridgeshire. The de Gerys began building on the site of the old monastery where they made their home for a number of years. This movement into Bedfordshire of families from other parts was by no means uncommon, although the majority came from neighbouring counties and from London. Richard Osborne, for example, was a successful London grocer who acquired the site of Chicksands and built his country house there.

Not all of the monastic sites and the plundered properties of the religious houses were developed immediately. It was almost a century before the Russells made use of the site at Woburn Abbey. Until the fear of plague drove them to the country in 1626, they preferred their town-house in London. Then the 4th Earl of Bedford put in hand the construction of an imposing ninety-roomed mansion, at that time the largest of the country houses of Bedfordshire. The new house had little agricultural land attached to it and Woburn park was less extensive than the one we know today. It stretched no further to the north than the public road that still bisects the park. At about the same time Sir Thomas Hillersden was considering the construction of a house on the old ruins of Elstow Abbey, just to the south of Bedford. He had acquired the estate from the Radcliff family who were related by marriage to the Herveys. Elisabeth Hervey had been the Abbess of Elstow from 1501 until 1524, and recent excavations have suggested that a house was built on the site soon after the dissolution, but that it was probably of little significance.[2] Shortly before his death in 1632 Sir Thomas Hillersden's mansion had arisen over the western half of the refectory and the whole of the western range of the monastery. But by 1781 Hillersdon Mansion was itself in ruins and only part of the porch of this E-shaped house remains. There we can still see the crest of the Hillersden family on the fragment of a building erected out of stone

[2] Baker, D., *Excavations at Elstow Abbey 1965-70* (1970).

robbed from the former abbey. South of the church runs a wide trough; it is the old carriage-way up to the front door of the house.

The St John family, having failed in their bid to secure Bushmead Priory, turned at the beginning of the seventeenth century to purchase the land at Melchbourne from the Russells. The land had been formerly used for a preceptory of the Knights Hospitaller, a site which Leland had described in the preceding century as:

> a right fair place of square stone standing much upon pillared vaults of stone, and there be goodly gardens orchards and ponds and a parke thereby.

Here the St John family built a dower house where 'The Cottage' now stands, and in 1610 they set about the task of building a new country home, having decided to abandon their existing seat at nearby Bletsoe as the house there was inconvenient, cramped and ancient.

Yet it was not just the new aristocracy of the two counties or ancient families such as the St Johns who had acquired monastic land who were to be found rebuilding their country seats during the seventeenth century. One of the largest and certainly the most majestic was Houghton House, begun about the year 1615 for the Countess of Pembroke. This elaborate brick and stone-dressed mansion like many others kept to a basic E-shaped plan, but its three storeys overall made it an imposing building. John Bunyan must have known Houghton House in its hey-day, when it was but a few years old. Today it is Bedfordshire's most romantic ruin. The roof has gone, but the mellow brick walls still stand almost to their full height in places (see Plate 18). The house enjoys a magnificent setting on the edge of the Western Lower Greensand scarp with wide views over central Bedfordshire. Houghton House was occupied for only a few decades. In the 1680s the Earl of Aylesbury, then its owner, fell foul of the political uncertainties that accompanied the reign of James II and he was forced to flee the country, whereupon 'that beautiful house that I doted on' was shut up. Later, Houghton House was purchased by the Russell family, but another tragedy came when the Duke of Bedford's son, the Marquis of Tavistock, was killed in a riding accident in the park in 1767. Before the century was over it stood gaunt and empty, an unroofed ruin.

Eastwards across the same county was the seat of one of the oldest of Bedfordshire's landed families, the de Greys of Wrest Park. They were to climb the social ladder when they became the Earls and Dukes of Kent. Like other important families the de Greys could not be outdone by the builders of the new mansions, although they were not inclined at first to rebuild all of their house. An inventory of the Tudor house in Wrest Park gives some idea of the level of comfort demanded by a landed family in the sixteenth century for the house included: 'the dining chamber, chapel chamber, my lord's chamber, my lady of Kent's chamber before marriage', together with a further seven main rooms plus 'the chapel, chamber over the storehouse, porter's lodge, chamber over the gate, clock chamber and clerk's chamber'.[3]

By Charles II's reign, however, the house was evidently too small and certainly unfashionable. An inventory for 1667[4] suggests that changes were taking place, for a new gallery overlooking the hall is mentioned. The detailed accounts have survived for much of the building work on this house and its successor, the present Wrest House, and in 1676 payment was made for the new front of the house.[5] Kip's fine engraving of *circa* 1705 shows us the new façade with the steep gables of the earlier house to the rear.[6] What is also of interest is the detail of the formal gardens (see Plate 19) with a 'Grand Canal' running from the rear of the

[3] B.R.O. L31/169.   [4] B.R.O. L31/170–8.
[5] B.R.O. L31/228.   [6] B.R.O. LL18/39.

house. The alteration of the gardens was as important as the house rebuilding in the seventeenth and eighteenth centuries and vast sums could be spent on reshaping to conform to the latest style. Between 1685 and 1701 over £3,000 was spent on the grounds at Wrest. Much of the expense went on labour, although over half a million bricks were also purchased, presumably for the park wall.[7] Another engraving, later in the eighteenth century (see Plate 20) reveals that the grounds have changed within a generation of the earlier drawing by Kip. A banqueting pavilion or house, built by Thomas Archer in 1711–12 has been added to the scene at the end of the main canal.[8] Part of this formal landscape still survives at Wrest, although the enlarged park was later modified by Lancelot 'Capability' Brown.

The concern with a pleasant, pastoral view from the main rooms of the mansion was not an innovation of the great eighteenth-century landscape architects. Although earlier parks were small and formal, the overall view was still important; in some cases the organisation and planning of that view involved the removal of 'offending' cottages. This had certainly happened at Conington by the beginning of the seventeenth century, for of the several houses pulled down by Sir Robert Cotton one was said to be against the terrace and garden of the house. Worse was to follow at Leighton Bromswold and Melchbourne where whole villages were destroyed solely in the interest of the landscaping of the big house. At Leighton Bromswold Sir Gervase Clifton began the building of a grand new mansion to the east of the church. Some doubt remains today as to whether the building was ever completed, although field-walking of the site in recent years has suggested that at least some of the main part of the house was finished. The only surviving building in the present landscape is a large gate-house, mainly of brick and dating from about 1616. The present

[7] B.R.O. L.31/288.
[8] J. Rocque, B.R.O. Z49/113 (1735).

village lies along the top of a ridge above the broad valley of the Ellington Brook, due west of the church. Its broad tree-lined street with the houses set back from the road at a regular distance gives a strong impression of conforming to an overall plan; it seems most likely that this replanning occurred at the beginning of the seventeenth century when the new mansion was under construction. The village of Leighton Bromswold formerly lay in a more irregular cluster to the south of the church and until recently the earthworks of the former house plots could be recognised in the fields. But the old village stood too close to the new house; consequently it was removed to the other side of the church, out of view. The church was also altered at this time by the Duke of Lennox, Sir Gervase Clifton's son-in-law who was Lord of the Manor of Leighton in 1634. He contributed money towards the rebuilding of the tower, but the fine interior fittings of the seventeenth century were the result of the efforts of George Herbert. The poet held the living, although it is unlikely that he ever visited the church from his home near Salisbury. It seems most likely that he took the advice of his friend, Nicholas Ferrar, whose small religious fraternity was established nearby at Little Gidding (see Plate 21). Both Leighton Bromswold and Little Gidding contain excellent examples of early-seventeenth-century woodwork, and the latter is still furnished in a college style with the seating facing across the nave rather than towards the altar and east window. Together they comprise the most interesting of Huntingdonshire's churches.

At Melchbourne the original medieval village lay to the east of the preceptory of the Knights Hospitaller. On aerial photographs you can recognise the house plots in the park of the hall. No documentary evidence survives to record the date of the removal of the village, but the mansion was built in the early seventeenth century and the row of picturesque cottages that stand outside the gate at the entrance to the park appear to be contemporary with it. They are among the earliest estate cottages in Bedfordshire. As at Leighton Bromswold, the prospect from the house was spoiled by the village. Melchbourne had to be moved to a more 'convenient' location.

But these landscape changes of the seventeenth century pale into insignificance when compared with the great expansion of landscaped parks and their resplendent houses in the following century. One of the earliest developments came at Kimbolton where the castle was extensively remodelled by Vanbrugh in 1707. Apart from the addition of an attic storey, his work survives intact (see Plate 10) and fragments of the earlier Tudor and seventeenth-century house can also be seen—mullioned windows in the south range, and the courtyard of 1690. Other landed families soon followed with large new houses. In 1747 the 4th Duke of Bedford commissioned Henry Flitcroft to rebuild and extend Woburn Abbey and it is his façade that we see today. A new house at Wrest might have predated Woburn by thirty years if family fortunes had not received a severe setback. In 1715–16 Leoni produced plans for the rebuilding of Wrest. When the Earl of Kent's son, Anthony, Earl of Harrold, was in Europe on the traditional Grand Tour he showed Leoni's scheme to Juvarra, the Court Architect at Turin. Juvarra criticised the design for its meanness and submitted his own, more elaborate, plan.[9] An estimate of £16,563 for the new house has survived, but it is not clear whether this was for Leoni's or Juvarra's design. The Earl decided to go ahead with rebuilding; in 1718 he announced plans to expand the park in order to provide a more fitting setting for the larger house. But in 1720 he lost heavily in the disaster of the South Sea Bubble and his town house in St James's Square, London, was badly damaged by fire. The Earl's heir, Anthony, died quite young in 1723, followed only five years later by the Duchess. The Earl was a broken man and

[9] Stated in a letter sent by Earl Harrold from Rome in 1715, B.R.O. L30/8/33/13.

abandoned any thoughts of rebuilding. The rebuilding of Wrest was not carried out until 1836 when the present house in a château style, designed by Clephane, was completed. The grounds, at least, had seen some change, for in 1758 'Capability' Brown was commissioned to landscape the park. Many of the clumps of woodland and the serpentine lake that surrounds the older formal gardens and canals are his handiwork.

The two great landscape architects of the eighteenth century, Brown and his successor, Humphrey Repton, were not particularly active in the two counties. Indeed, Huntingdonshire has scarcely any evidence of their work. Brown had the largest number of commissions. He was responsible for the parks at Southill, Luton Hoo, Ampthill and Wrest although Repton had the largest single task in the landscaping of Woburn Abbey. Brown's work at Wrest has already been mentioned. The straggling lake is not a good example of Capability Brown's treatment of landscape because he had to work with part of the park—the canals— already fixed as the focal point for an expanse of water. Brown was fond of damming streams in order to provide a shallow lake in front of the main rooms of a house and he was able to do this very effectively at Luton Hoo where the River Lea was widened in its passage through the park. Repton did not favour this method of 'improvement' and at Woburn he created instead a string of small lakes in front of the house. Both landscape architects were, however, devoted to planting 'natural' clumps of trees, although when Brown came to manage the landscape at Ampthill he was able to make use of the many great oaks that still existed in the royal hunting park that had been the delight of Henry VIII.

Titled families were not the only ones to indulge in major schemes of rebuilding in the two counties and a number of smaller Georgian houses, their styles rather closer to the town houses of the period than the grandiose efforts of the very wealthy in the countryside, can still be seen in the landscape. Bedfordshire's two finest examples are Eggington and Hinwick House. The former (see Plate 22) was built in 1694, its strict classical style pointing to developments that were to become dominant several decades later. Like a number of other smaller houses of the gentry Eggington is built in brick. It was the home of the French Huguenot family of Reynal or Renouille, a family who aspired to the position of Sheriff of Bedfordshire. Hinwick House was another early house, built by Richard Orlebar in 1710 for his bride, Diana Astry. The pediment contains a carving of the goddess Diana in her honour. Elsewhere, houses were being added to or given a new façade in the current style and their small parks were being expanded. Flitwick manor was enlarged in 1736 and the grounds landscaped soon after. Following Brown's example the insignificant stream of the Flit was damned to create a wide canal at the southern end of the park. By the end of the century the owners had succeeded in diverting the road that used to run in front of Flitwick manor so that it was realigned to the north of the church.[10]

The enlargement of the parks during the eighteenth century often involved much more than a mere road diversion. At Wrest the expansion of the park in readiness for the new house, a rebuilding that was to remain only a dream, involved encroachment upon the fields of the hamlet of Ion. The hamlet has since shrunk to the farms of Great Ion and Ion Farm, to the south-east of the park. Wrest park also expanded northwards into Clophill parish where the land there was of little value for the sandy soil only supported a rabbit warren. Upper and Lower Gravenhurst were also to lose some of their land to the same park. The growth of Woburn Park northwards beyond the minor road that enters past the church was more serious in its consequences. Not only did it destroy some of the fields of Husborne Crawley,

[10] This can be seen on maps of 1717 and 1793, B.R.O. LL17/338 & R1/250.

but soon after 1760 it saw the disappearance of half of the houses of the village. A map of 1760 shows the village of Husborne on either side of the road—the present A418— but today the park wall now follows the east side of this main road and the houses have vanished completely.

By the end of the eighteenth century there was a significant concentration of large mansions, each within its landscaped park and surrounded by a high wall, in a narrow belt of countryside that stretches across central Bedfordshire. It is not difficult to see that this aristocratic belt corresponds closely with the dry, infertile soils of the Lower Greensand, the same region in which there was still room for expansion of cultivation in the Middle Ages and where many of the later deer parks could also be found. The Geological Survey of Great Britain notes that where the Greensand deposit is thick and not covered with drift, as at Rowney and Old Warden, the percolation of water down to a low water table has led to the development of small ravines and steep slopes, too poor for profitable agriculture and yet most suitable for the development of dry parkland. Today much of the area is still unsuitable for anything else other than woodland and the great parks lie interspersed between belts of coniferous plantations. On the eastern side of Bedfordshire's Greensand the parks of Ickwell Bury, Old Warden and Southill form a continuous north-south line of parkland that is over three miles in length and about ten miles in circuit.

The estate village and farm

The great estates grew through the eighteenth and nineteenth centuries by the careful acquisition of smaller landed properties as they came onto the market. Marriage too was a valuable means of estate expansion. Land agents kept a careful eye on individual farms or even the property of entire villages that might prove suitable additions to the estate. As a result the number of owner-occupiers was reduced and there was a corresponding increase in the number of tenant farmers. It was the culmination of a pattern of engrossment that had continued unabated since the end of the fifteenth century. Although the engrossment of estates was widespread over most of the country, it is noticeable that it had a greater effect in Bedfordshire—where the larger estates were to be found—than upon Huntingdonshire. Farmhouses and cottages were rebuilt to conform to the new estate style, a rebuilding that usually meant an improvement in living conditions to a level above that of other homes which lay outside the estate. Although part of the thinking behind such improvements was based upon the Victorian principle that a man would be more content and work harder if his home conditions were satisfactory there were a number of wealthy non-conformist landowners who considered the management and development of their properties in a rather different way. Such was the case at Cardington in mid-Bedfordshire where fine eighteenth-century houses around the little green are the result of the reforming zeal of the Howard and Whitbread families. The rise of the Whitbreads from obscurity to wealth and prominence amongst the country's landed gentry is perhaps characteristic of many individuals and enterprises that saw the establishment of Great Britain as the major industrial workshop of the eighteenth-century world. Samuel Whitbread was not an industrialist, but had worked his way to the top in a London brewery until he was able to control it completely. His son, a second Samuel, had amassed enough wealth to purchase Southill Park in 1795, the former home of the Byngs. The park had already been landscaped by 'Capability' Brown in 1777 and Whitbread commissioned Brown's son-in-law, Henry Holland, to redesign the house. Here indeed was a revolution in society: that a brewer could aspire within one generation to the position of great landowner and that he was able to afford the services of the same builder as the Duke of Bedford! It was not long before the

149

Duke was to find that the Whitbreads were being considered for county posts which had always been the perquisite of the Russells and other old county families. While the house was being rebuilt at Southill the cottages in the adjoining village received similar attention, being reconstructed in an attractive new style, with low thatched roofs and elegant dormer windows. Many of them survive (see Plate 23), some with circular plaques upon their walls bearing the date of completion and the initials of Samuel Whitbread. Other later houses, in different styles, also show the continuing interest of the family in their workers' accommodation throughout the nineteenth century.

Although the Whitbread estate was to be the second largest in Bedfordshire, by the third quarter of the nineteenth century it was the Bedford estate of the Russells that continued to dominate the scene. From a small nucleus around Woburn Abbey in the sixteenth century the estate grew northwards and eastwards, encompassing much of the former Honour of Ampthill and even acquiring land in the extreme north-west of the county. Further afield substantial areas of the Cambridgeshire and Huntingdonshire fenland came to the family as a result of their interest in the seventeenth-century schemes for reclamation in the Fens. Over a large part of central and western Bedfordshire the sight of the rather plain semi-detached houses of the Bedford estate is still a common one, in village and town and in a large number of isolated farmhouses. Most of these properties were the result of rebuilding in the middle of the last century. Around the centre of the estate, in the villages of Husborne Crawley, Lidlington, Ridgmont and Willington the dominant influence of the dukes of Bedford and their agents is still obvious in the large number of older properties that still bear the single letter 'B' on their walls accompanied by a small coronet, the symbol of this aristocratic family. But even in isolated Souldrop, one of the outlying parts of this fairly compact estate, the same effect can still be recog-

nised. At Ampthill the growth of the Bedford Estate's influence in a small market town can still be seen in the rather
plain façades of the nineteenth-century houses (see Plate 24).

If the houses of the Bedford estate are no more inspiring
than the majority of council houses in the twentieth century,
the same could not be said of some other estate villages
where their owners chose to adopt an elaborate and picturesque style. Many of them have an individuality and
rustic charm about them which makes them very attractive
properties and those that have been released onto the market
have often realised unusually high prices. At Old Warden,
for example, the Ongley family of Warden Park created a
delightful group of cottages in brick and honey-coloured
stone with thatched roofs and delicate porches built of
uncut timber (see Plate 25). This English Garden style was
emulated in a number of places. At Brampton, near Huntingdon, Lady Olivia Sparrow built a number at Brook End,
but none can rival the scale of Old Warden.

The owners of the great estates not only designed and
built villages, they were also active in the rebuilding and
restoration of churches. The 'estate' church of the nineteenth century has become a distinctive element of the
English landscape. The de Greys, for example, had by
tradition been buried in the church at Flitton and the Grey
mausoleum occupies the east end. Silsoe Church, although
it stood just outside the gates of the de Greys' park, had
been a chapel of ease to Flitton. In 1829–31 it was faithfully
rebuilt in the Perpendicular style by the architect Smith of
Hertford as an estate church. At Southill the Whitbreads,
never staunch Anglicans, nevertheless paid for a new roof,
seats, screen and window in 1814–16. The greatest of the
new churches was, however, at Woburn where the 8th Duke
of Bedford commissioned Henry Clutton to build a church
to the east of the small town of Woburn and alongside the
drive into the park. This huge church is hardly of village
proportions but it was after all intended for a duke. The

Duke's correspondence, which can be seen in the Bedford-shire county record office, makes it clear that he was little concerned with expense and rather more with the design features of his new church. Clutton built in the style of the late twelfth century, although it is clear that he was strongly influenced by French style of that period as much as English.

Those who dwelt in the new cottages built by the great landowners may not have realised how fortunate they were to enjoy reasonably comfortable living conditions; certainly those who lived elsewhere were less well provided for. In 1793, in his report to the newly formed Board of Agriculture, Thomas Stone noted that there was a shortage of 'comfortable cottages' for the poor in Huntingdonshire. This shortage, however, was also partly attributable to the great estates where landowners operated a closed village policy. In order to keep the number of labourers to a minimum, and hence reduce the risk of a high levy of the poor rate to support labourers and their dependants, land-owners kept a strict control on the number of new houses allowed in the village. Stone reported that as a result farmers were forced to import labourers for the harvest.[11] It appears that villages where a closed village policy was not operated were swollen by estate workers as a result. Poor rates were certainly of their highest in the unenclosed parishes and, as we shall see in the next chapter, these were also character-ised by a lack of overall control by one or two large land-owners.

SELECT BIBLIOGRAPHY

Camden, W., *Britannia* (first published 1595, later revised by Edmund Gibson). Facsimile reprint 1971.

[11] Marshall, W., *Review and Abstracts of the County Reports to the Board of Agriculture from the several agricultural departments of England,* Vol. 4 (1815), p. 402, David and Charles reprint. n.d.

Godber, J., *Wrest Park and the Duke of Kent* (Henry Grey, 1671–1740), Bedfordshire County Council, 2nd Ed. (1975).

Godber, J., *John Howard the Philanthropist,* Bedfordshire County Council (1977).

Hoskins, W. G., *The Age of Plunder* (1976).

Prince, H., *Parks in England* (1967).

R.C.H.M. (England), *Huntingdonshire* (1926).

Stroud, D., *Capability Brown* (1975).

Thirsk, J. (Ed.), *The Agrarian History of England and Wales,* Vol. IV, 1500–1640 (1967).

6. The agricultural landscape, 1450-1700

Early agricultural improvements. The final clearance of the medieval woodland. A great rebuilding.

Early agricultural improvements

NO MATTER HOW we view the condition of the manor in the middle of the fifteenth century, it was not what it had been in 1300. The relationship between lord and villein had been irreversibly changed by the vicissitudes of the economy in the fourteenth century. The villein emerged as a copyholder, still bound by the rulings of the manorial court but no longer tied to the soil of the manor. Work services had in many places been reduced to a money rent and a greater freedom was allowed on some manors in the exchange of land. As a result demands began to be raised for the enclosure of strips in the open fields as individual farmers sought to create more viable holdings.

Although changes are evident in the rural society and economy of these times, late medieval and Tudor manorial court rolls make it plain that many manors were seeking to maintain the status quo. There had been attempts in the past to exchange holdings in the open fields without the lord's consent, as the late-thirteenth-century rolls for Chalgrave illustrate, but it is noticeable that the manor was then in a position to withstand the pressures for change, and the size of holdings and their scattered disposition amongst the open fields remained remarkably static. But by the middle of the sixteenth century the situation was transformed as the court rolls for Caddington, a parish on the Chalk in south Bedfordshire, illustrate.[1] Over some fifty years there is abundant evidence that piecemeal enclosure was occurring in the open fields. In 1546 George Ferrers, gent., and Thomas Bray, senior, were accused of enclosing part of the common fields; Ferrers had converted ten acres to the enclosed Mallows Croft while Bray had turned sixteen acres into Bowsers Close and Little Taylors Field. In 1569 Richard Mershe enclosed a hundred and fifty acres of common field of Caddington and the court recorded that over three hundred acres had been enclosed in the parish within the previous twenty years, adding the rider that most of it had gone in the past four. Caddington was clearly in the process of changing its medieval patterns of farming and there is little evidence that the fines imposed by the court had much effect. Even the lord's waste or common grazing land was not immune, for in 1602 ten persons were named:

> which have digged and plowed upp the lords waste shall remove yt away and make the grounde agayne smooth before Christmas Day.

In view of the great number of encroachments that had already occurred on the common land of the manor it is again doubtful if the court's ruling was adhered to. What remained of Caddington's open fields was swept away in the parliamentary enclosure of 1798 and much of the parish now has the characteristic field boundaries of hawthorn hedges that were a common feature of such enclosure. But in the north of the parish, around Zouches Farm, the fields are smaller and have a more irregular outline suggesting that they were part of the open field that had been enclosed earlier.

There is evidence from other manorial courts, and associated documents, for early enclosure, but the two counties did not see a great deal of it. Many parishes, particularly

[1] *Caddington Court Roll 1546–1602*. B.R.O. CRT Caddington I.

those of the heavy clays, remained in open-field cultivation until the end of the eighteenth century. When early enclosure occurred it appears to have been the result of a strong control of the manor over the parish, a result usually of the single ownership of land. At Bletsoe in mid-Bedfordshire the entire parish was enclosed in the early seventeenth century. The Manor of Bletsoe had been the seat of the St John family from the middle of the fifteenth century until their removal to Melchbourne about the year 1610. With their movement they had evidently decided upon the agricultural improvement of both parishes. A manorial survey for Bletsoe was undertaken 'uppon the newe inclosure and finishing of it Anno D'nni 1624'.[2] The only pieces of common land to survive were the tiny greens that acted as centres of the scattered population outside the village, notably Whitwickgreen (or Whitwick End), Boln End, Coplowe Green and North End. Whitwickgreen had lost some of its common grazing for the survey mentions a number of new houses upon the green. It is an intriguing aspect of the survey that these small hamlets were also occupied by freemen and not copyholders, surely a reflection of the way they had been established earlier in the Middle Ages as outlying knots of pioneer settlement in the woodland.

At Melchbourne the St Johns enclosed a large area of common land that must have involved much of the parish's open fields at that time. The details are unfortunately not as full as for Bletsoe, but in 1679 Lord Bolingbroke was said to have enclosed about nine hundred acres.[3] Many of these enclosures have now been lost in the later expansion of Melchbourne Park and its great backcloth of plantation woodland. But these are early and rare examples of the transformation of Bedfordshire's medieval landscape; few other enclosures were complete by this stage. Woburn was already enclosed when the Russells had an estate map drawn

[2] B.R.O. CRT 110/34.   [3] B.R.O. CRT 130.

in 1661[4] and seventeenth-century maps of the western half of the huge parish of Eaton Socon reveal a number of small enclosed fields. In Huntingdonshire a few of the landed gentry were keen to encourage early enclosure of the open fields but this did not always go through unopposed. A protracted legal case ensued over the Cottons' enclosure of common land which involved blocking the right of way over Little Gidding Common to Sawtry. The chief protagonist in the dispute, which lasted from 1647 until 1659, was 'Mr Ferrar' of Little Gidding.[5] Similarly at Keyston the Duke of Manchester's land in the southern half of the parish had been enclosed at an early stage but the rest of the parish, being outside of the Lordship, had refused to alter its methods. These open fields were still in existence when the Tithe Map was produced in 1839 and the narrow, intermixed strips were not finally removed until the very late date of 1850.

The most active of the enclosers in Huntingdonshire were the Cromwell, alias Williams, family. Having acquired a large portion of the former estate of Ramsey Abbey at the dissolution they were busy by the middle of the seventeenth century in reducing the number of open fields on several of their manors. At Broughton in 1648 an agreement was reached between Sir Richard Williams, alias Cromwell, and the tenants of the manor for the voluntary enclosure of their fields. But when the estate changed hands in the following year the new owners, James Ravenscroft and William Hetley, who held the reversion, were less keen on the change and the tenants were forced to take the case to Chancery before the matter was settled.[6] Although Broughton has suffered as much as anywhere in the county in recent years from the removal of hedgerows, quite a number of these early enclosed fields can still be recognised, particularly in the south of the parish.

As in Bedfordshire, an assault was also being made upon

[4] B.R.O. X1/33/1.   [5] H.R.O. CON 5/1/2.   [6] H.R.O. 15/219.

the areas of common grazing. The manorial court at Brampton was most concerned in 1635 and again in 1644-45 with attempts to enclose part of the common. A 'Mr Peeps', father of the more famous Samuel and a holder of land in the parish, was fined two pence for setting his 'poles' upon the waste of common.[7] But a much larger onslaught on the wastes was being carried out further east, in the peats of the fenland. The Huntingdonshire fen was composed almost entirely of peat and was frequently affected by fresh-water inundation from the great rivers—most notably the Great Ouse. The economy of the fens had depended on wild-fowling and fishing, and the grazing of herds of cattle when marshes and peaty swamps dried out in the summer months. But this was all to change under a grand scheme instigated by the 4th Earl of Bedford and a group of men prepared to 'adventure' their capital in reclaiming large tracts of common land in return for a share in the land. They engaged the Dutch drainage engineer, Cornelius van Vermuyden, and he began the cutting of a major dike or drain in 1630 as the main part of a plan to divert the waters of the Great Ouse from its meandering course, to ensure that floodwater could reach an outlet in the Wash more rapidly. Although much of the land that was to be reclaimed as a result of the plan lay in Cambridgeshire, the cutting of the new drain began in Huntingdonshire at Earith and cut straight across the fen for over twenty miles before rejoining the Ouse at Denver. The Old Bedford River remains a major feature of the landscape of the fens today. At its southern end, in the pasture between the Old and New Bedford Rivers—the latter begun soon after the first when it became apparent that one drain was insufficient—lie the remains of a small redoubt of the Civil War, the Bulwark, a reminder that the major works of reclamation had to struggle through many years of strife and uncertainty. Two other cuts were made in Huntingdonshire as part of this grand scheme of regional

[7] B.R.O. M60/8.

reclamation—the Forty Foot or Vermuyden's Drain, which improved part of the west fen around Ramsey and carried the water into the Old Bedford River, and Bevill's Leam, which carried water eastwards from the great lake of Whittlesey Mere.

A number of the Adventurers who were also Commissioners of Sewers already had an intimate knowledge of the vagaries of the fen and the ever-present peril of flooding. The Commissioners of Sewers had overall responsibility for ensuring that fen drains were scoured and defences repaired. The new reclaimers worked closely with the Commissioners and so it is not surprising to find some men belonging to the two bodies. One such person was Sir Robert Cotton. He began his own scheme for the reclamation of Conington Fen as early as 1639. The eastern half of the parish stretched onto the peat fen; there the Monks Lode to Sawtry Abbey had defined its eastern boundary for centuries. The canal had been constructed between 1161 and 1179 and allowed the monks to bring in supplies of building stone as well as providing an outlet for trade through the open water of Whittlesey Mere. An early estate map for Conington, dated 1595, shows an empty marsh around the Lode, although those parts of the fen that lay closer to the village were already enclosed and in use for pasture. Sir Robert's new enclosures took in the parts of the parish between the Lode, New Dyke and the farm called Eternity Hall.

The initial success of the reclamation of the peat fen was apparent to all except those who had made their living from fishing, fowling and gathering reeds in the wild, unenclosed fenland. But it was not long before major problems were encountered as the new drains proved to be inadequate; wind pumps were slowly introduced to raise water into the major water courses from an ever shrinking fenland. Much of the Huntingdonshire fens remained unreclaimed for severe problems were posed by the deep meres of Whittlesey, Ramsey and Ugg, problems that were not to be solved until the introduction of powerful steam-driven pumping engines in the middle of the nineteenth century. Even where land had been reclaimed it often remained in use as pasture. Richard Cromwell, son of the purchaser of the Ramsey estates, was leasing 'fenn closes' as early as the late sixteenth century—in 1586–7—in the old common fens of Ramsey, Bury and Hignay (part of Wood Walton Fen) with the strict condition that they should not be tilled. Later Cromwells were keen to enclose the fen commons and in 1629 and 1653 they made agreements with the tenants of Ramsey for the enclosure of large areas of fen to the north and east of the town. The first included Stocking Fen and the one hundred and eighty wax seals attached to the agreement reveal the large number of people who held a right of common grazing there. These commoners were to give up their rights, together with those that they held in nearby Much-wood Chase, in return for a small parcel of land.[8] Muchwood Chase can be identified today with Muchwood Lane, east of Stocking Fen. In 1629 it was still substantially wooded for the agreement referred to the removal of 'trees, deere and coneys'. Stocking Fen is still divided into small rectangular pieces of land, a symbol in the modern landscape of its early drainage and enclosure. The same is true of most parts of the common fen that was the object of the second agreement. That involved the reclamation and division of 'The Hollow, Long Beach, Puddock Mere, Drapers Delph, Ryshills, Skeggings, Thistle Green, Mid-Fetter, Broaddale and Broadealls Halt' and more of 'Stockinge Fen'. Most of these names can still be identified in the landscape. Skeggings, for example, is Skeggins Fen, north of Bodsey House and alongside the old course of the River Nene. Beyond the river, and therefore some distance out in the fen, can be found Mid-Fetter Farm amidst a group of small, rectangular fields. Even further out is Drapers Delph, an odd triangle of ground bounded on one side by the old Nene channel,

[8] H.R.O. R1/2/1.

on another by Monks Lode and with Ugg Mere formerly on its south side. In a similar isolated position but on the eastern side of the huge parish of Ramsey (including the nineteenth-century parish of Ramsey St Marys which was carved from it) lies the district of Broadall. A tongue of firmer land runs north from Ramsey town to the southern edge of a large common, now divided into narrow rectangular plots. The junction of the two lies at the Forty Foot drain and the agreement of 1653 makes mention of this new canal.

Most of the early enclosures, whether of open common field or of extensive fenland common grazing, were part of a general improvement in agricultural methods. The agreements in the fenland parishes involved the whole of the community but elsewhere enclosure was often a piecemeal enterprise. Although very few open-field parishes were completely enclosed during the seventeenth century, many others produced a pattern of partial enclosure. Few were in the position of the Manor of Upton, which embraced the whole parish, when its fields were surveyed in 1659. The map[9] (see Plate 26) shows three great open fields with all the settlement of the manor neatly contained within a compact village. Practically all of the waste land had been used by that time and only the trees of Upton Wood remained together with a common on the eastern edge of the parish.

At Hockcliffe, straddling the main road of Watling Street in western Bedfordshire, the reasons for the enclosure of the entire parish were specific and rather unusual. A document in 1620 recorded that the enclosure had recently taken place because the open fields were:

spoiled and trodden with cattle, sheep, park horses and hackneys, because of the nearness thereof to a high road called Watling Street and because of the driving of cattle to and from Leyton [Leighton Buzzard] and other places

[9] H.R.O. C4/2/21/1.

by which means the parishioners were much damaged before the enclosure.

Roads in the seventeenth century were in a parlous state for they had no road metalling other than stone and gravel that might be obtained from the locality. Their upkeep was the responsibility of individual parishes. Watling Street was a much used major route to the north-west of the country in the seventeenth century, and the parish of Hockcliffe must have found it an impossible task to cope with the damage caused by heavy traffic. In winter, when one part of the road became impassible, travellers often trespassed onto the surrounding fields and the width of the road might well have stretched over a hundred yards as a result of innumerable diversions. Hence the reason for the enclosure, to contain the road users and ensure that crops were not spoilt. The mention of cattle in this seventeenth-century document from Hockcliffe is also significant for this was one of the roads used by the Welsh cattle drovers who took their beasts to the London market. One suspects that Hockcliffe farmers were also very concerned about such herds being allowed to roam across the open fields. However, the cattle drovers made their impact upon the area for some fields were used as pasture and several local farmers turned to cattle rearing. As late as 1854 Kelly's Directory records a John Green as landlord of the White Hart at Hockcliffe who had another trade as well, that of cattle salesman. Earlier, in 1669, a Welsh drover boy travelling to the market at Smithfield had died on the way and the Hockcliffe burial register records that he was buried in the parish.

Another important drove road can be followed across Huntingdonshire, parallel to the Great North Road from the border with Northamptonshire and the Soke of Peterborough down to a junction with that road at Alconbury. The Great North Road was turnpiked in 1662 and the charging of tolls must have turned many of the cattle

drovers to the alternative route of the Bullock Road. This
droveway survives in part as a minor road, in others as a
broad green lane and at its northern and southern end only
as a footpath or hedge line. It is remarkable for its great
width, far wider than most of the other roads in the district
that are the product of the parliamentary enclosures in the
eighteenth century. The best stretches run through Folksworth and Washingley parish and along the edges of the
parishes of the three Giddings, Sawtry and Glatton (see
Plate 27). Some indication of the great age of the Bullock
Road can be gleaned from the way in which the route often
follows the boundaries of parishes, suggesting that the parish
boundary, when it was established at the end of the Dark
Ages, was able to make use of a previously established line
—in other words a trackway dating from the depths of
prehistoric time was already there (see Fig. 9).

On Elton Furze the continuation of the Bullock Road can
no longer be followed northwards on the ground, but
Thomas Jefferys' map of the county, printed in 1768, shows
the line it took to the crossing of the Nene at Wansford.
This is the same drove road that W. G. Hoskins has traced
towards the River Trent at Newark, surviving in part as a
green way, the Log Drift or Sewstern Lane, along the
boundary between Leicestershire and Lincolnshire.[10]

Several farms which stand on or close to the drove road
betray the purpose of the route in their names. Coldharbour
Farm occurs twice within a few miles, in the parishes of
Steeple Gidding and Folksworth with Washingley, a name
quite frequently to be encountered along ancient cattle or
sheep droves. On the high ground of Great Gidding parish,
close to the drove road, can be found Flittermere Lodge.
The pond from which the farm takes its name has now
disappeared but it was surely a watering place for cattle on
the move. Nearby, the drove road encounters the Northamptonshire boundary for a short distance at Moonshine

[10] Hoskins, W. G., *Fieldwork in Local History* (1967), pp. 144–5.

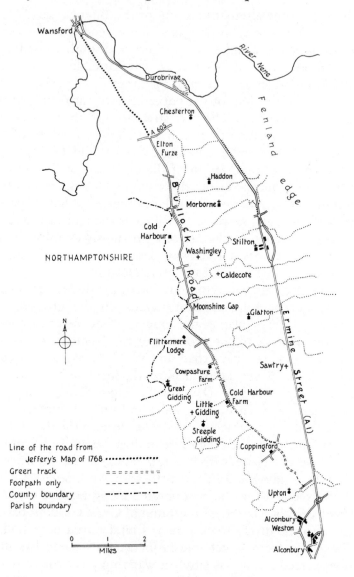

Wansford

River Nene

Durobrivae

Chesterton

F
e
n
l
a
n
d

A 605

Elton
Furze

Haddon

Morborne

e
d
g
e

B
u
l
l
o
c
k

Cold
Harbour

Stilton

Washingley
+

R
o
a
d

+Caldecote

Moonshine Gap

+Glatton

NORTHAMPTONSHIRE

N

E
r
m
i
n
e

Flittermere
Lodge

Cowpasture
Farm

Sawtry+

S
t
r
e
e
t

Great
Gidding

Cold Harbour
Farm

(A1)

Little
+Gidding

Steeple
Gidding

Coppingford

Line of the road from
Jeffery's Map of 1768 ••••••••••••
Green track   ===========
Footpath only   ----------
County boundary   —-—-—-—-—
Parish boundary   ·············

Upton

0   1   2
Miles

Alconbury
Weston

Alconbury

Fig. 9. The Bullock Road.

164

Gap and what more evocative name could there be for this isolated little piece of country where great herds of cattle were driven through day and night to feed the London market. Cattle would need to be fed as well as watered en route and drovers must have been anxious to reach recognised pastures alongside the road. Most of the Huntingdonshire parishes traversed by the road were still in open field arable at the end of the eighteenth century, but where earlier maps survive they reveal small closes of pasture alongside the droveway. John Hausted's map of Glatton (1613) shows a number of these closes among the open field strips of West Field and Berye Field; they were obviously used by the cattle drovers. The present footpath that runs from the village to Moonshine Gap was known as Lutton Slade and appears to have been another drove road if we are to judge from its great width today and its seventeenth-century name. Close to the Slade and Moonshine Gap was Denton Pond, another watering place beside the Bullock Road. An eighteenth-century map of the former parish of Washingley also reveals the Bullock Road crossing an area of pasture in the vicinity of Ongutein Manor (then called Packs Lodge).[11]

The final clearance of the medieval woodland

The seventeenth century saw the end of most of the surviving fragments of woodland that had escaped the axe of the woodcutter of the Dark and Middle Ages. Timber had become scarce by the seventeenth century and this fact is reflected in the widespread introduction of stone and brick for vernacular buildings in many parts of the two counties. In north-west Bedfordshire and western Huntingdonshire whole villages were rebuilt or refaced in the local Jurassic stone, of which Stevington and Elton are among the finest examples. Across central Bedfordshire small brickworks

[11] H.R.O. Estate map of 1753. TLR 468.

seemed to spring up everywhere and the smaller farmers began to replace their timber-framed houses in the new material. Heavy oak frames were slowly succeeded by flimsy scantling and more often than not timber came from outside the county.

The last fragments of Weybridge Forest were cleared rapidly after 1600, when the covenant that preserved the district in a natural state for hunting came to an end. A map of 1651[12] shows that the Earl of Manchester still held over three hundred acres of woodland in the old forest, half of it in six enclosures which stretched north from Weybridge Farm to the minor road that runs from the A1 to Woolley. From the names given to the enclosures it is clear that the woodland was being regularly coppiced. But by 1672[13] the great forest had nearly all gone and the coppiced enclosures were no more. Only on the very western edge of the parish (Alconbury) did a wood survive and even there inroads had been made, for that which formerly stretched into Ellington parish had become 'Ellington ploughed ground'. Elsewhere in the county of Huntingdon the story was the same and by the end of the century the only remaining woods of any size were Brampton and Warboys Wood. In Bedfordshire some of the ancient tracts of woodland were to survive a little longer for they formed part of the resources of the Bedford estate of the Russells. In the north of the county Odell Great Wood and Knotting West Wood (see Plate 6) have altered little over the past three hundred years, at least as far as their area is concerned, but the rest of Knotting parish is now empty of the wood that used to cover large areas on the east. In 1646 several hundred acres of woodland extended across into Melchbourne but just over a hundred years later that had been considerably reduced in size. Today the boundary is completely bare. Further south, on the scarp of the Lower Greensand at Houghton Conquest, Bury Wood

[12] H.R.O. SM 3/17.
[13] H.R.O. SM 3/18 (estate map).

still covered seventy acres in 1595, but by 1635 it was already described as partly 'stubbed up' and its location is only remembered by the name of Bury Farm.[14]

The detailed maps produced by Thomas Jefferys in the middle of the eighteenth century and Bryant's survey of Bedfordshire in 1826 provide valuable information about the extent of surviving woodland. In spite of more than a thousand years of clearance, it is noticeable that the Lower Greensand still supported some considerable woods. The greatest concentrations occurred in western Bedfordshire on the Bedford estate, centred on Woburn and Souldrop. The correspondence of a nineteenth-century land agent makes interesting reading with regard to the management of the woodland. In a review of a thirty-year period in the first half of the nineteenth century Thomas Bennett noted that the north Bedfordshire woodland had contained the greatest number of oaks but that they had suffered the greatest decline in recent years, leaving only 860 acres of usable woodland.[15] Too much attention had evidently been paid to the underwood, to the detriment of the timber itself, as a result of the demand for temporary fences in the open fields and also at the time of their enclosure, for under-draining and for fuel for the poor and for bake-houses. After enclosure, however, demand for temporary fencing fell, clay pipes were replacing wooden ones as field drains and coal was coming into widespread use as a fuel. As a result, the agent had ordered the grubbing up of poor woodland and its conversion to farmland which was to be added to adjoining farms. Thirty-seven acres of Twin Wood, Clapham, were disposed of in this way, while at Knotting the removal of Bourn Wood, Home Wood and Hernehoe entailed conversion of almost another two hundred acres. Where the timber still had a commercial value, however, the Duke and his agent were keen to tap new areas of demand. In 1835,

[14] B.R.O. RO 5/256 and 261.
[15] Correspondence held in the B.R.O. (Russell papers).

having heard of the building of the London to Birmingham Railway, the Duke was endeavouring to dispose of timber from his estate to satisfy the huge demand for sleepers. In the previous year oak bark had been sold to a Birmingham firm and a few years later there was the possibility of supplying oaks from Woburn Park to shipbuilders on the Thames.

The landscape of Bedfordshire and Huntingdonshire on the eve of the great phase of parliamentary enclosure late in the eighteenth century must have been as devoid of trees and hedges as at any time in the long history of its evolution, although the recent rapid removal of hedgerows over the last two decades has come perilously close to reproducing that same landscape. In those parts where arable agriculture reigned supreme the eye could have roamed across great open spaces, unbroken by wood, hedge or isolated farm. By the early years of the nineteenth century parliamentary enclosure had done much towards adding fresh detail to this empty landscape, as we shall see in the next chapter.

A great rebuilding

Some mention has already been made of the new building materials of brick and stone that were becoming available to the small farmer by the end of the seventeenth century. But for the more prosperous yeoman farmer, the man who had amassed an estate of some hundred acres or more, the sixteenth century was an important time when his newly acquired wealth enabled him to rebuild or add to his existing home. To understand what form this rebuilding took in the landscape one need look no further than one step up the social hierarchy, at the new houses of the squires and country gentry, to see that social betterment involved copying the styles—often at a distance—of those above you. Hence the Tudor farmer's image of a new house was the late medieval manor, with its open hall. By the end of the sixteenth century tastes had changed; the new trend was for a hall that had been partitioned and divided into two floors, with service wings at one or both ends, the common L, E, and H-shaped plan that typifies so many of the buildings of both yeoman and wealthy landowner (see, for example, Plate 18 for the E-shaped house of Houghton Hall). The Manor House at Brington, Huntingdonshire, is a good example of the smaller house of the middle of the century, constructed in timber and still having the open hall. But even this house that looks back to the late Middle Ages was not built without any refinement for the stone chimneystack appears to date from the start of the building; there was no question therefore of an open hearth. The hall was not divided up until the late seventeenth century. As it stands today it has an L-shaped plan but the original house had two side wings; only that to the west now remains. Further north in the county, close to the Nene, Manor Farm, Orton Waterville is a fine example of a new house, built with hall and cross wings in 1571. It is rather unusual for the use of stone rather than timber at this early date. M. W. Barley has suggested that when a yeoman took over the farming of the manor's demesne the manor house began to be known as Manor Farm and in a number of cases, such as Orton Waterville, a new house was provided. Although the hall in this case was still following a medieval plan, the two floors of the cross wings again reveal how the new styles have been incorporated.

Timber-framed houses of the sixteenth century are not very common in the two counties, certainly not as thick on the ground as further east in Norfolk and Suffolk or to the south in Hertfordshire. One wonders whether this is a reflection of a lower level of prosperity or a result of the growth of the great landowner and the absentee landlord from an early date that excluded the yeoman farmer. We have already noted that Huntingdonshire formerly had much land in the hands of the monasteries and most of this had passed straight into the possession of the new Tudor magnates at the dissolution. Some good examples can be found, such as the early sixteenth-century Lime Tree Farm, Wistow and Moat Farm, Marston Moretaine, but the vernacular traditions of the two counties are much better represented, as far as the small- and medium-sized farmer are concerned, by the seventeenth century.

Many of the new houses of the seventeenth century were in the centres of the villages. They represent an improvement of living conditions not only for the farmer but also for the cottager, the labourer and the craftsman. Their houses are simpler than those of the wealthier yeoman and they represent a clear break from the medieval tradition that was centred upon the hall. They are built around a central chimney-piece, without service or cross wings on one or both sides. These were relegated to a position at the rear, often added under a low sloping roof or out-shut. The timber framing was frequently hidden behind layers of plaster. Such houses can be recognised in almost any village or hamlet of the two counties, although in the stone areas of the north and west it is often difficult to detect the earlier examples of a building style that was to persist for several centuries. Timber framing persisted for a long time, and in some places a very early tradition, that of the cruck-frame, can still be recognised, at Husborne Crawley for example and at Manor Farm, Clipstone. Such timber-framed structures are rare in eastern England and there has been much recent discussion as to whether they represent the survival of a form that was once extensive and that was swept away by the introduction of newer techniques or was the cruck-framed structure always more popular in the west and north of England, where the best examples are now to be found. I am inclined to favour the first of the two arguments and to see their existence in Bedfordshire today as a reminder of an old tradition that has been replaced several times over through the past four centuries. This argument of renewal could perhaps also be extended to the sixteenth-century yeoman's house for there are examples of seventeenth-century farmhouses—as in the villages of Alconbury and Alconbury Weston—that appear to be almost complete re-buildings of an earlier house in which the chimney-piece or a small section of framing are the only parts of an older house that have been retained.

Although the seventeenth century witnessed a return to the use of brick, it was often in combination with a timber frame. Moat Farm at Marston Moretaine has brick infill or nogging within the heavy timber frame and this form of building is by no means uncommon amongst early farmhouses. In some cases the bricks were set diagonally in a herringbone design. Only in the larger houses, the halls and manors are solid brick houses to be found, as at Toseland Hall. The manor house at Warboys (see Plate 28), adjacent to the churchyard, is an excellent example of a three-storeyed gentleman's residence with its double-gabled front given a distinctive element in the Dutch style of the brick gable ends. In its position on the edge of the fen Warboys must have had frequent contacts with Dutch traders and Dutchmen were of course involved in the reclamation of the peat fen during that same century.

SELECT BIBLIOGRAPHY

Alcock, N. W., 'Timber framed building in North Bedfordshire', *Bedfordshire Archaeological Journal,* 4 (1969), pp. 43–68.
Barley, M. W., *The English Farmhouse and Cottage* (1961).
Darby, H. C., *The Draining of the Fens* (1940).
Mercer, E., *English Vernacular Houses* (1975).
Pevsner, N., *The Buildings of England: Bedfordshire and the County of Huntingdon and Peterborough* (1968).
R.C.H.M. (England), *Huntingdonshire* (1926).

7. The rural landscape in Georgian and Victorian times

Parliamentary enclosure. Settlement growth and decline.

Parliamentary enclosure

BEDFORDSHIRE AND HUNTINGDONSHIRE were still predominantly open field counties in 1750; only in a few places had there been voluntary agreements for the enclosure of open fields, yet by 1850 practically all the old arable strips and furlongs had been swept away and replaced by a regimented pattern of rectangular hedged fields, through which ran long straight roads. This new Georgian landscape—for most of it was accomplished before Victoria's reign had begun—still dominates the scene over large parts of the two counties. Across central Huntingdonshire the monotonous fields run for mile upon mile, interspersed at intervals by small, nucleated villages, distinctive for their twisting lanes and irregular closes of an earlier period. At Great Catworth, for example, the broad and straight enclosure road that approaches the village from the north suddenly narrows and twists as it climbs the hill to the village, and the edge of the parliamentary fields is quite clear. On the west of the road the broad ridges of the former open field can still be seen, a fossilised medieval pattern underlying the new hedged landscape of the late eighteenth century. The break between old and new enclosures can be well observed on the northern outskirts of St Ives, where the road to Pidley and Somersham follows a twisting route as it leaves the environs of the town and its closes until it reaches Marley Gap Bridge. The bridge marks the edge of the great heath that was inter-commoned until its enclosure in 1796. Until that date an old coach road crossed the heath to the former palace of the Ely bishops at Somersham, but the enclosure commissioners laid out a new road, one that runs dead straight for over three miles. The farms along this new road and elsewhere on the heath all post-date the enclosure, and their mid-Victorian styles suggest that they were not constructed until some time after the laying out of new fields.

Before the passing of the General Inclosure Act in 1750, enclosure had been carried out through a private agreement between landlords and tenants, although some had sought the ratification of Parliament. This appears to be the case for Sutton in Bedfordshire, in 1741, when an Act was secured as confirmation of an agreement having been made and which gave power to enclose without the need of a Commission. During the reign of George III the pressures mounted for a widespread encouragement of enclosures and the enabling legislation of 1750 was followed by a great increase in the number of parishes seeking their own Acts. Something of the turmoil that this must have produced can be gauged from the reports of the various gentlemen appointed to report to the newly formed Board of Agriculture. In 1794 Thomas Stone said of Bedfordshire that there was still a considerable number of parishes in open field cultivation, together with pastures and wastes. It is interesting to note that Michael Williams' analysis of the extent of waste land in England and Wales in or about 1800 —derived from the County Reports—reveals that Bedfordshire had a very high proportion of such land, as a percentage of the total county area, when compared with any other county in lowland England. Bedfordshire's 38.7 per cent is in marked contrast to the 7.1 per cent of Northamptonshire, the 1.3 per cent of Buckinghamshire, and even Huntingdonshire, given its fenland tracts, at 9.0 per cent. The statistic for Bedfordshire's waste land leaves a clear impression of the infertility of the Lower Greensand.[1] Most of this wilderness still existed when Thomas Batchelor produced his report in 1808, but he stated that fifty enclosures of open field had occurred since 1794 and only forty-three of the one hundred and twenty-four parishes remained unenclosed. In Huntingdonshire similar progress had been made; there George Maxwell reported only forty-one of the one hundred and six parishes enclosed in 1794, but by 1811 R. Parkinson states that two-thirds of the county was wholly enclosed.

In spite of the considerable quantity of contemporary literature that was available extolling the virtues of enclosure, the individual Acts make little mention of why the decision was finally taken. What is clear, however, is that the decision was made by the landowners and not the tenants. The preamble to the Kensworth Award of 1798, when approximately half of the parish—some 1200 acres—were to be enclosed, stated that:

the said land and grounds lay inter-mixed and disposed in small pieces or parcels and in their situation were incapable of any considerable improvement and that it would be beneficial to the several persons interested therein if the same were divided and allotted to and amongst the several proprietors.

In this part of South Bedfordshire reaching up to the Chalk the 'considerable improvement' would almost certainly have involved conversion of some of the arable to pasture. This region of Bedfordshire was favoured by cattle and sheep farmers who were expanding their acreage to satisfy the growing demands of the London market for fresh meat. And it would seem that much of the enclosure of open fields in northern Huntingdonshire was for a similar reason.

[1] Williams, M., 'The enclosure and reclamation of waste land in England and Wales in the eighteenth and nineteenth centuries', *Transactions of the Institute of British Geographers,* 51 (1970), pp. 55–70.

It is noticeable that only a few benefited directly from the enclosures at Kensworth and this was the case in the majority of parishes. In particular, the Huntingdonshire parishes that succumbed to enclosure had only small populations, most of them below 500 in the Census of 1801 and several with fewer than a hundred inhabitants. Not only were their populations small, but landownership was in the hands of one or two proprietors and only a few tenant farmers were engaged in cultivation. Contemporary writers believed that enclosure had further reduced the number of farms in Bedfordshire in the second half of the eighteenth century (Thomas Batchelor, 1808). There can be no denying that the period saw a decline in the number of farms but whether it can be attributed to enclosure is debatable. The engrossing of farms since the sixteenth century can be recognised as a common feature, and while enclosure may have accelerated the process it is unlikely to have been a major cause in itself. Indeed, the evidence for the two counties is that much of the engrossing and the disappearance of the smaller farmer was over before enclosure took place; in many parishes the land could hardly have been held in fewer hands on the eve of their particular enclosure. A few examples from the documents of the period can be used to prove this.

The parish of Denton was enclosed in 1802, by which time there were but four proprietors concerned: Thomas Wells, the largest landowner who held substantial estates in central Huntingdonshire, John Nichols, S. A. Apreece—of nearby Washingley Hall, but holding only a tiny portion—and the Rector. The land was tenanted out to a handful of farmers. Yet a survey of some thirty years previous revealed that the pattern had changed little, although the tenant farmers were a slightly larger body in 1770.[2] When one considers the highly fragmented character of the holdings of those few farmers, it is not difficult to understand the

[2] H.R.O., Denton Inclosure Award and a Survey Book of 1770 Acc. 54.

reasons for enclosures at Denton. Caldecot Furlong, for example, covered 41 acres but it was divided into 158 lands; Glatton Side Furlong had 175 lands. At nearby Upton the open fields covered the whole of the parish in the seventeenth century apart from a piece of land in the east that was devoted to the Common and the ancient Upton Wood (Plate 29). It was these open fields, three in number, that were swept away by the enclosure of 1812. But then there were only four landowners although one of them, John Heathcote, had several tenants (see Plate 35). However, even this small number of proprietors were more than the usual number of landowners in parishes where enclosure had come early and where communities had become engulfed within one of the great estates. Single ownership was the rule in places affected by early enclosure. Maxwell's County Report for Huntingdonshire noted that the large proprietors were to be found holding the parishes in the old enclosed parts of the county and Batchelor states that the largest farms in Bedfordshire were to be found in the south and east, the area of the great estates. North of the Ouse the 'poor clay soils' had apparently acted as a deterrent to the 'opulent farmers'.

Those who engineered the enclosure of the open fields also had to meet the cost of the whole procedure. For a large landowner this could be very considerable and one wonders whether it was also a factor in explaining the reluctance of parishes dominated by small proprietors—and there were some, notably on the edge of the fen—to hold back from enclosure until a very late stage. John Heathcote noted down his expenditure incurred with the Upton enclosure of which the total came to £396 6/-. It involved seeing the Act through Parliament and paying the expenses of the commissioners and a surveyor. But even after the Act had been passed his expenses continued for he was required to fence his new blocks. The Act of Inclosure usually required fencing to be complete within a year. For Upton, Heathcote paid £76 in 1812 for 320,000 'Quicks', quickset or hawthorn saplings, paying a further £25 in the following year.[3] And there is still abundant evidence in the fields of Upton of John Heathcote's new hawthorn hedges.

The commissioners were able to allocate land in large blocks when only a few proprietors were involved. Most of these blocks were far too large for either pastoral or arable use and one suspects that part of Heathcote's large expenditure on saplings was in order to divide his blocks up into more manageable units. The commissioners were not concerned with the most convenient size of fields—and that would vary with purpose—but simply with a fair reallocation of the scattered strips. Most parishes were quick to subdivide their blocks into smaller fields, and it is this last act of the revolution of enclosure that we find imprinted on the landscape today. Where pastoralism dominated in the new economy, such as around the small villages on the upland clays of central and northern Huntingdonshire, fields were divided into units of ten acres. This was the ideal size suggested by the pamphleteers who were promoting improvements in stock rearing at the end of the eighteenth century. At Spaldwick, for example, the enclosure of Spaldwick Lordship produced an enclosure map, dated 1775, of large blocks. But another map, produced in the following year shows already that the process of subdivision was well advanced. Although there has been a revival of arable farming in the area in more recent years, parts of Spaldwick are still under permanent pasture, as they have been since the open fields were enclosed.[4]

The enclosure of the open fields often meant the extinction of tithes and this in itself widened the gap between the large landowner (where he was the impropriator of the rectorial tithe) and the smaller proprietors who used to pay tithe upon their produce. The abolition of tithes was accompanied by

[3] H.R.O. C4/2/20/2.
[4] H.R.O. 1775, PM 4/7 & 2230/55. 1776, SM 17/113.

compensation and although the tithe had been ten per cent of certain produce the amount of land given up was normally nearer twenty per cent. The argument behind the surrender of such a large portion of land to the tithe holder was that the tithe would now be regarded as a net rather than a gross return from the land and as the tithe holder would incur costs in farming the land then a larger share than ten per cent was justified. The inevitable result was to widen the gap between large and small proprietors. In the same way the manorial lord received compensation for giving up his rights to the areas of common grazing. In many cases, because the manorial lord was the holder of tithes, he would see a substantial increase in his share of the land as a result of enclosure. Sometimes one of the Oxford or Cambridge colleges might be involved for they too had benefited from the redistribution of land after the dissolution of the monasteries. At Kensworth the huge Common was destroyed by enclosure. 113 acres went to the Dean and Chapter of St Pauls, as holder of the impropriated rectorial tithes, and William Howard, holder of the vicarial tithes, and lord of the manor, received over a hundred acres of the former common land. The Common extended southwards from the present B4540 road to the woodland on the boundary with Studham and eastwards down the hill to encompass Kensworth Lynch. Part of the new fields have since been built upon, but it is still possible to recognise some of the old farmhouses and cottages that stood on the northern edge of Kensworth Common before enclosure.[5]

The enclosure of the Common added a new element to the landscape of several parishes in the early years of the nineteenth century. The new roads across the enclosed commonland often left farms and cottages in isolation marking the former edge of the Common. This theme is illustrated at Stanbridge, one of the hamlets of Leighton Buzzard which was not enclosed until 1840. A small tri-

[5] B.R.O. Map MA98/2 and Award, 1798.

angular piece of common land still exists by the church, but it was formerly much more extensive, stretching southwards to the River Ouzel at Stanbridgeford. At the time of enclosure houses on the western side of the Common were given long closes that led down to the new road. Some of those cottages still survive; they once marked the edge of Stanbridge Common but their closes have been given up to more recent housing alongside the road. The same process has happened at Sawtry where Green End has been joined to the rest of the village by the recent expansion of housing estates. In 1612 Green End was a separate element in the morphology of Sawtry parish; fourteen houses were scattered around the edge of a small common. The outline of the green can now only be found with difficulty for the enclosure of 1809 created a number of small, rectangular fields and these have since been sold off for housing development. Here and there, amongst the new houses several buildings of the seventeenth and eighteenth century can still be recognised.

After the enclosure of the open fields and the commons a few farmhouses began to be built away from the village. Before enclosure many parishes consisted of a nucleated village where hardly a farm or farm building was to be found standing out in the fields. This is still true for the settlement pattern of a large part of Huntingdonshire. Few landowners could afford the expense of moving their dwelling house to a convenient site in their new fields immediately after enclosure. John Heathcote's accounts provide an illustration of how little the settlement pattern of Upton was affected by the enclosure of 1812. In 1813 he paid for the erection of two cottages and barns for B. Wheatley and Bateman but this financial transaction seems to have no direct connection with the enclosure of Upton and there is no suggestion that the buildings were placed anywhere other than in the existing village. Wheatley's cottage was to be built of materials taken from the demolition of another Upton property. In the following year another new cottage was provided by John Heathcote, but again it appears to have occupied a site within the village. Only in 1819 is there reference to an isolated site when 5,000 bricks were purchased for the 'new cottage at the wood'. Upton Wood must be the place in question for there was no other woodland remaining in the parish by that time. Even so one cannot be certain about the location of this cottage; there is no evidence for a cottage there today and the Tithe Map also shows an empty area. Only one farm at Upton lies outside the confines of the village and that is Upton Lodge. It was a late addition to the settlement landscape and was certainly not a direct consequence of the 1812 enclosure. Only at nearby Stukeley did John Heathcote make a note of providing a new barn for one of his tenants as a result of the new allocation of fields. Enclosure occurred in 1813 and by 1815 the tenant, who unfortunately is not named, had a barn removed 'to his new allotment'. Even here it seems unlikely that his house was also removed.

In other places some new post-enclosure farm building can be recognised, but they are exceptions to the general pattern of no-change that followed the reorganisation of farming with the enclosure of the open fields. At Little Catworth, for example, we can be certain that Bunkers Hill Farm was erected very soon after the enclosure of the parish in 1781. Elsewhere the names of farms that commemorate contemporary events help to indicate the gap that occurred between enclosure and rebuilding. For instance, Waterloo Farm at Offord Cluny must have been built some twenty years after the enclosure of 1794. But such names are very rare in the landscape of the two counties; far more frequently we find the 'lodges' and 'glebes' whose Victorian houses reflect the influence that the great landowners and clergy held among the proprietors of farmland. Mention has already been made of Upton Lodge. A mile or so to the south-west lies the joint parish of Barham and Woolley whose open fields were enclosed before 1780; yet only Woolley Lodge and Lodge Farm interrupt a monotonous landscape of rectangular fields. Glatton, a larger parish, now has seven farmhouses out in the fields where only one (now known as Ermine Lodge) existed before enclosure. There, the debate over enclosure went on for eleven years and it was only drawn to a conclusion in 1820. The enclosure documents mention nine proprietors by name together with 'several other persons' who were presumably of so little consequence that there was no need to name them. After enclosure it is noticeable that only Thomas Wells, lord of the manor, and the clergy were able to afford new farmhouses out in the fields. Perhaps Gibson's Hovel, a cottage to the east of the village, represents one of the smaller proprietors?

Georgian farmhouses form part of the landscape of Bedfordshire and Huntingdonshire but their presence, even in an area of parliamentary enclosure, does not necessarily mean that the houses stand in lonely sites remote from the parent village. At Marston Moretaine in central Bedfordshire enclosure came in 1796. There, Beancroft Farm is certainly a fine example of a late Georgian farmhouse. But a moat surrounds part of the site, proof that a farm had been there for several centuries before the erection of the Georgian house at the time of the enclosure at the close of the eighteenth century.

Despite the number of great estates and mansions in the two counties, fox hunting never seems to have played a significant part in the recreation of activities of the country gentry, at least not so significant as to affect the landscape through the planting of fox coverts. Here the landscape of enclosure is different from that of other counties in the East Midlands. On the borders of Northamptonshire and Buckinghamshire a few coverts can be seen in the parishes of Steeple Gidding and Turvey. At Southill alone they appear to have been an important element in the new fields,

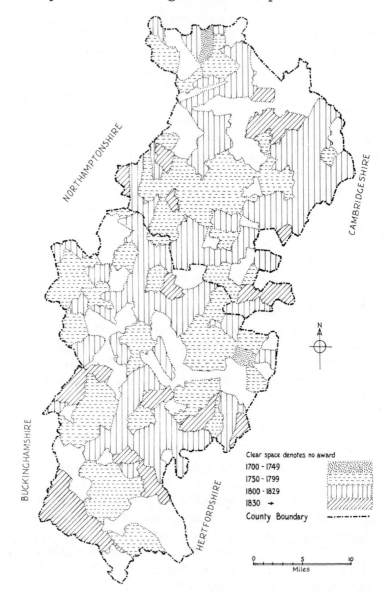

Fig. 10. Enclosure Acts of the eighteenth and nineteenth centuries.

surviving as small triangular copses between the hamlets of Broom and Stanford and clearly visible from the B658 road.

By 1820 most of the open-field parishes were enclosed (see Fig. 10) and even some of the great areas of common grazing, whether of heath or fen, had been divided up amongst individual commoners. In the parish of Ramsey, for example, Herne and Gore Commons were enclosed by 1801, producing a landscape of small, narrow fields that were divided up amongst the many individuals who still held grazing rights. A number of new cottages appeared on these allotments. Lotting Fen, to the south of Ugg Mere, was also enclosed at this time. Here the large numbers holding common rights resulted in a minute division of the land. But the disappearance of the fields brought about an economic revolution that was as important as the new hedged landscapes. The tithe maps of the 1840s reveal a region of pastoralism across Huntingdonshire and much of Bedfordshire north of the Ouse—all classic areas of parliamentary enclosure. Only on the Lower Greensand did arable remain dominant, while in south Bedfordshire dairying, with the emphasis on butter and cheese for the London market, had taken a strong hold.

Settlement growth and decline

With the commencement of the official Census in 1801 we are able to recognise those parts of the two counties where population growth was rapid and where it was in decline. Although the population of both Bedfordshire and Huntingdonshire showed a steady increase throughout the nineteenth century much of the growth happened in the towns or rural areas where particular specialisms were developing, notably in market gardening and brick-making. Elsewhere many parishes began to show a decline from the 1840s onward.

Market gardening began at Sandy in east Bedfordshire in

the early years of the seventeenth century, when William Springe, described as a 'gardener', had purchased an acre of land. The term 'market gardener' or 'market garden' does not appear to have come into common usage until the nineteenth century so we must recognise earlier references to the trade through the records of the produce grown and the names given to fields, such as 'carret ground' or 'rhedish (radish) ground'. A glebe terrier for Sandy in 1708 describes a piece of ground 'lying on the south side of the great barne commonly called the Rhedish ground and always in the occupation of a Gardener'. Frank Beavington in his study of the development of market gardening in Bedfordshire has located twenty-five references to market gardening between 1610 and 1700 at Sandy, with a further thirty-one between 1700 and 1750. Yet the open fields of Sandy were not enclosed until 1798–9, and the fifty-five acres of old closes that existed on the eve of enclosure could not have supported the total acreage that Beavington believes to have been in use for market gardening. Consequently this intensive and specialised form of farming must have taken over some of the land in the open fields of the parish. Proof of this may be found in a number of land transactions and the wills of market gardeners in the seventeenth and eighteenth centuries. It is clear that Chester Field, to the south of the village where the former Roman settlement lay, was the focus of market gardening. While Chester Field may once have formed part of the common open fields, it is clear that by the time the land was used for market gardening it was no longer part of the communal arrangements of Sandy's open fields.

It is not at all clear why market gardening should have developed at Sandy at such an early date. The local demand for market garden produce must have been negligible in the seventeenth and eighteenth centuries. Sandy was only a village and the towns of Bedford and Luton could only muster a population of 7,000 between them in 1801. Such small towns would have certainly provided enough from their own local gardens. But the London market was large and growing at a rapid pace. The turnpiking of the main road from the north to London through Biggleswade was to give a great boost to Sandy. There were toll gates to the south and north of Sandy and an analysis of their receipts over the period 1725–63 shows a big increase in traffic through the southern gate but with only a modest increase in a northern direction. Most of the increase was of waggons and carts, carrying garden produce, root crops and cucumbers, to the London markets.

The growing of intensive crops began at Sandy on the alluvial rich terraces of the River Ivel, but as demand increased market gardening spread onto the sandier and poorer soils of the Lower Greensand, where levels of productivity could only be maintained through liberal applications of manure. The gardens extended into adjacent parishes and by the early nineteenth century Old Warden, Biggleswade, Clophill and Maulden were all specialising in root crops. At the time of the enclosure of Sandy's open fields some 60 acres were given over to market gardening; only ten years later 150 acres were under specialised crops. But the most substantial increases in acreage were to await the arrival of the railway.

Market gardening encouraged the continued growth of population at Sandy through the nineteenth century. From 615 at the First Census in 1801 there was a sharp increase within twenty years to 1178, a total which had more than doubled by 1881. The other villages engaged in market gardening showed considerable increases of population but none were as dramatic as Sandy's. But elsewhere in rural Bedfordshire the general trend in the latter half of the century was towards decline and stagnation. Beavington has estimated that whereas most communities in the central parts of the county showed a decline in their population of between 30 per cent and 40 per cent during the period 1871–

1901, the market-garden parishes were able to hold their own and Sandy increased by 25 per cent.

In south-west and central Bedfordshire a number of villages benefited from the manufacture of straw plait in the early years of the nineteenth century, the plait being made up by women and children for the developing straw-hat trade of Luton and Dunstable. Unfortunately the demand for local plait declined in favour of cheaper material from the Far East by the middle of the nineteenth century. The population of many of the villages fell as females in particular began to migrate to Luton to find employment in the hat trade. Straw plait provided only a temporary additional source of income and employment in the rural areas. With the growth of brickworks, however, came employment that was to be permanent in many places. The evolution of brick-making as an industry is best left to another chapter, but it is worth while examining the influence that small brickworks made upon population levels in the nineteenth century.

Apart from the villages in central Bedfordshire and those around Fletton in north Huntingdonshire, where the manufacture of bricks is still centred, it was the fenland edge parishes that were to benefit most from the expansion of this industry. Around the edge of the peat fen are patches of clay that produce the creamy yellow bricks which form one of the most characteristic elements in the landscape of the fenland villages. At Warboys, alongside the disused railway station and on the very edge of the fen, a specialist brickworks still functions but elsewhere all that remains is a number of shallow, grass-covered pits and the cottages that formerly housed those who worked in the clay-pits and kilns. At Ramsey Heights, alongside the road that runs west to the Wood Walton Nature Reserve, a number of depressions are the only surviving evidence in the countryside of the brickworks of the middle of the last century. Kelly's commercial directory for 1854 records two traders at

Ramsey Heights who were engaged in brick making, and it is interesting to note and a measure of the small scale of their activities that they both had another occupation. John Summers was also a beer retailer and one suspects he must have done well in such thirsty work as brick making! George Harris combined his trade with that of farming.

All of the fenland edge parishes record increases of population in the second half of the nineteenth century when the rest of the county was showing a clear decline. Some of the expansion can be attributed to brickworks, as at Ramsey Heights, but some also came as a result of further reclamation of the fen and the consequent expansion of arable land. Although much of the peat fen had been reclaimed during the seventeenth century, several large tracts still survived in their natural state. Indeed, when Britten and Brayley produced a topographical account of Huntingdonshire in 1808 they estimated that of 44,000 acres of fen in the county only 8–10,000 acres were productive. One of the chief reasons for the limited area of reclaimed fenland devoted to productive farming was the imperfect drainage. Britten and Brayley claimed that the productive acres were themselves unprofitable as a third of the rents had to defray the expenses of protecting the land from further inundation. The parts of fenland that had been left by the reclaimers, presumably because they found them too difficult, consisted of a number of shallow meres. Several such sheets of water were to be found in the huge parish of Ramsey, particularly Ramsey Mere and Ugg Mere, but the largest of them all was Whittlesey Mere in Glatton and Holme parish. It was over two miles across at its widest point and covered 1570 acres in the 1780s when a detailed map was produced. Whittlesey Mere was used for fishing and wild-fowling; during the winter ice-skating was also popular and in the summer it was frequented by 'parties of pleasure'. It was the yachtsmen who had been as opposed to the drainage of the mere as those who made their living from it. Work finally began on reclamation in 1853. Today it is hard to trace out the shape of Whittlesey Mere, the regular grid of fields making it look no different from those parts reclaimed two hundred years before. The boundary of the lost mere can however be partly reconstructed by recognising that Mere Mouth Farm stands on its northern edge. It can be followed across the fields (although the actual margin is now obliterated) to Frog Hall, Johnson's Point and Ladyseat Farm. Each of these were on the edge of the mere when John Bodger made his survey in 1786. Within the area of the reclaimed mere only four farms were established: Black Ham, Tower, Iron House and Engine Farm, the last named on the site of one of the great beam engines that were an essential part of the mid-nineteenth-century fenland landscape and which helped to keep the mere dry after it had been drained (see Fig. 11).

Ramsey Mere and Ugg Mere were also drained in the middle years of the nineteenth century and their former existence is again marked by a number of farms. Only one farm was built on Ugg Mere, Wellington House; several new holdings, including Mere Farm, were sketched out on the floor of Ramsey Mere. The old course of the River Nene acted as the western boundary of the mere to the north of the town of Ramsey. Its eastern edge can still be recognised by the long curving ditch that divided the mere from Broadall Common. The reclamation of the meres expanded the cultivable area of the fenland parishes, and the number of men required in reclamation must also have given a considerable boost to employment in the area. As the fen became more suitable for arable crops—a change greatly aided by the building of branch railway lines in the second half of the century—settlement spread onto the peat lands in a way that had not been seen before, even in those parts where reclamation had been successful in the seventeenth century. The First Edition of the One Inch Ordnance Survey still shows the fens largely empty of settlement and

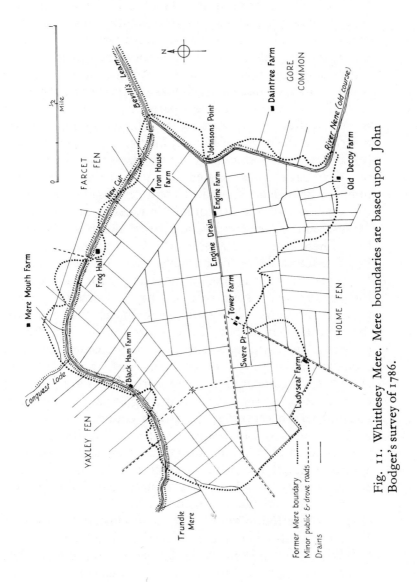

Fig. 11. Whittlesey Mere. Mere boundaries are based upon John Bodger's survey of 1786.

this early-nineteenth-century evidence is corroborated by that of private estate maps and the slightly later tithe maps. Yet by the middle of the century fresh farms and cottages had sprung up along the long, straight new roads. Some settlements still favoured sites upon the old abandoned water courses or *roddons*. Such was the growth of Ramsey's fenland population that a new parish had to be created out of the western part, Ramsey St Marys. Another parish emerged to the north of Ramsey at Pondersbridge. The red brick Victorian Gothic church at Pondersbridge, built when the new parish was created in 1866, stands at a major junction of fenland roads just south of Bevill's Leam. But the grandeur of the Victorian churches is at Ramsey St Marys. Built of the local yellow brick alongside the Forty Foot Drain (the old course of the Nene at this point), its huge structure defies the unstable peat on which it stands. However, the fen has already taken its toll for the tower no longer supports a spire that had to be dismantled as the foundations sank. This grand, new church was provided through the beneficence of a Ramsey woman, Mrs Emma Fellowes, in 1858; two years later a separate civil and ecclesiastical parish was created. Such new Anglican churches are comparatively rare in the peat fen for by the time of the active settlement of the region in the eighteenth and nineteenth centuries, the parish churches on the surrounding upland had assumed responsibility for the scattered fenland population but were not inclined to provide a separate church for them. It was left to the non-conformists and particularly the Methodists to fill the gap. Until this day the peat fen has remained distinctive for its large number of chapels to be found among the small clusters of farms or along the roads where the peculiar fen villages stretch over a distance of a mile or more. Some are now disused but several of them have found fresh uses, often connected with servicing the local farmers as agricultural repair workshops and the like. A few stand forlorn and derelict, too isolated to be of value to anyone. Such is the chapel to be found at Toll Farm, Ramsey Hollow.

The fenland parishes increased their population throughout the middle years of the nineteenth century, but a very different picture is preserved by the clay-land parishes of north-west Bedfordshire and west-central Huntingdonshire. The Census Returns show that the decades of the 1820s and 30s mark the peak period of maximum population for many of the villages in those areas. Some villages are still declining at an alarming rate in the twentieth century. Steeple Gidding, for example, had a population of 93 in 1821, a total only once more exceeded in 1881 when it reached 125, but by 1971 it had fallen to 43. Barham and Woolley were separately counted in 1821 but their joint total—the maximum for the century—was 168; but by the last census in 1971 they had fallen to 71. Many of Bedfordshire's villages have revived within the past two decades as they have become popular places for the new homes of Bedford's growing commuter population, but in common with those in Huntingdonshire they had suffered particularly badly in the second half of the nineteenth century. It is not easy to establish with any certainty the factors responsible for this rural decline, but the initial causes might well have been associated with overcrowding in some of the villages. Many communities have grown too rapidly in the first few decades of the nineteenth century, at a time when both arable and pastoral farmers were shedding labour. Growth was focused on certain settlements because in several places a 'closed village' policy was in operation. Thomas Stone's remarks in 1793 about 'a shortage of comfortable cottages for the poor' must have rung true for many labourers in Huntingdonshire. In many parts of the two counties evidence can still be seen in the landscape of the effects of overcrowding upon the housing stock. We find houses with additional entrances, a result of the subdivision of accommodation. Again, there are extra chimneys and lean-to's or outshuts. Former yeomen's farmhouses, no longer serving their original purpose after the purchase of their lands by the greater proprietors, were divided to house two or more families.

Improved methods of transport in the nineteenth century made a considerable impact on rural communities, even if they did nothing more than re-emphasise their isolation. Small market towns continued to grow while the villages around them declined and although the early decades of the Census Returns do not provide sufficient details, it looks as though the towns were expanding at the expense of the villages. The smallest and most remote settlements had been hit the hardest by the middle of the century. But all rural areas fell into a decline in the last three decades of the century when the 'Great Depression' of British agriculture hit the two counties. By 1912 an agricultural survey noted an area of 'rank scrub, hawthorne and wild rose' said to stretch continuously from Everton to Tempsford that had taken the place of former arable land. This was the area of the Lower Greensand and the clays to the north where arable farming had persisted when other districts had changed over to pasture a century earlier.

With the decline of the rural population a number of hamlets and small villages passed out of existence. For a long time some of them had been on the verge of extinction. In truth several of the so-called 'deserted medieval villages' were not completely extinguished until the nineteenth century. Little Catworth, for example, was still a living community at the end of the eighteenth century. The hamlet consisted of two rows of farms and cottages, but now only a couple of houses and a patchwork of uneven ground in the fields on either side of the long lane that goes nowhere betray the site of the once active settlement. Only two miles to the east of Catworth lies the lost hamlet of Upthorpe. In 1775 twelve houses still stood there but by the 1830s only three remained.[6] All that is left today is the widening of a cart

[6] Spaldwick Inclosure Map (1775), H.R.O. PM 4/7 & Spaldwick Tithe.

Plate 28 The Manor House at Warboys is an excellent example of the use of brick by some of the country gentry in the middle of the seventeenth century.

Plate 29 Detail from the Upton enclosure map of 1812 shows how far land-ownership had become concentrated into the hands of a few by the early nineteenth century. John Heathcote dominating the parish. Comparison with Plate 26 might suggest that the village had also declined since 1659.

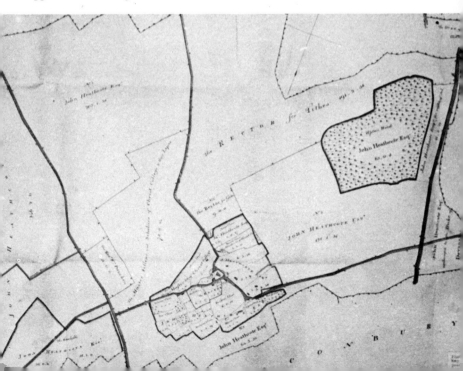

Plate 30 Glatton village in 1613. John Hausted's excellent map is the finest of Huntingdonshire's early maps, detailing the open fields and closes with their owners and acreages, all in rich colours. But a walk through the village today will reveal a number of gaps where houses once stood, for it has declined over the past three centuries.

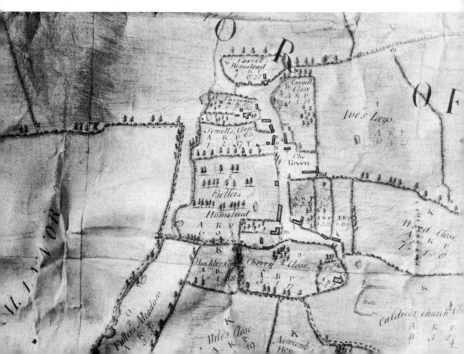

Plate 31 Steeple Gidding in 1648. Now a deserted village, apart from a disused church, a farm and a couple of cottages, this map makes it clear that decline had not occurred in the late Middle Ages, when conversion of arable to sheep pasture ruined so many villages in the Midlands.

Plate 32 Caldecote near Folksworth in 1753. 'The Town' of this now deserted village can be clearly seen and it is clear that, like Steeple Gidding, decline has been very recent. Another part of the same map reveals the neighbouring village of Washingley already deserted.

Plate 33 The Bell Inn at Stilton, reputed home of the famous cheese, was built in the middle of the seventeenth century on the site of an older inn in response to the increase in coach traffic. The Cotswold stone frontage is more characteristic of Northamptonshire than Huntingdonshire.

Plate 34 The grim landscape of the brick pits of central Bedfordshire is a vivid reminder of the huge expansion of brick making in the area with the coming of the railways in the middle of the last century.

Plate 35 Water Newton Mill on the River Nene is typical of the watermills along the Nene and Ouse whose existence posed a serious hindrance to navigation. Although most of this structure was rebuilt in the eighteenth century there is evidence that it was in existence from a much earlier date; there were two mills recorded in Domesday Book.

Plate 36 The market place at Harrold now looks no different from any village green, apart from the attractive eighteenth-century open market hall built at the height of the pillow lace industry.

Plate 37 A remnant of the hatting industry of Luton. The small workshops characteristic of the trade can still be seen in Frederick Street Passage.

Plate 38 Skefco Works, Luton. The Swedish ball bearing company still retains a site alongside the railway to the north of the town centre, a location that was all important in 1910 but has little significance today; the original frontage has been replaced.

Plate 39 A Land Settlement Association estate at Wyboston. Like the pioneer settlement at Potton this still thrives as a private estate of smallholdings, with its distinctive feature of regular spaced houses all built to a standard design.

Plate 40 A mixed residential and industrial landscape at Heath and Reach reveals the change that has come over this area of former wood and heath in the past fifty years. The extraction of fine silver sand for glass-making and tiles was begun by the Marley Tile Company in the early years of this century and suburban growth from nearby Leighton Buzzard has created a haphazard and untidy scene that is all too common in the present landscape.

track near to Upthorpe Lodge and the grass-grown platforms of abandoned buildings. Stoneley near Kimbolton and Boughton hamlet, between Southoe and Diddington, both show a similar pattern of desertion in the first half of the nineteenth century.

From an analysis of the tithe and enclosure maps for central Huntingdonshire and north-west Bedfordshire, it is clear that many of the platforms of abandoned homesteads that occupy the gaps within the village street-lines of the twentieth century belong to the Victorian period rather than the desertions of the late Middle Ages. Where a compact settlement once stood, now a more open-space pattern can be seen in the villages of Haddon, Morborne, Denton, Old Weston, Hamerton, Knotting and many others. Each began to lose population from the beginning of the fourth decade of the nineteenth century; today they are shadows of their former selves (see Plate 30).

In some villages we find only a few cottages and a disused church. At Steeple Gidding, for example, the empty church stands at the end of a lane with only a farm and a couple of cottages beside it. Gone is the manor house, its earthworks clearly recognisable in the pasture to the south-west along with the sites of a number of other houses. Steeple Gidding was still a populous place in 1648, so conversion to sheep pasture cannot be blamed for its demise (see Plate 31).[7] Then there were sixteen houses on either side of the lane but by 1841, when the tithe map was produced, only those on the northern side had survived. The fields on the south still bear the clear marks of former occupation. Caldecote, close to the deserted site of Washingley, is an even better example of late abandonment. Its tiny church survives down the lane that leads to Manor Farm and several houses have been built in recent years, but of the nineteenth-century village nothing is left. The process of shrinkage appears to have occurred between the middle of the eighteenth century and the 1850s.

[7] H.R.O. SM 18/120.

In 1753 an estate map was drawn covering much of Wash-ingley and Caldecote.[8] 'The Town' of Caldecote is clearly shown with houses on either side of the lane and the field to the north-east, where signs of desertion can still be recog-nised, forming part of the homestead closes. By 1847 the township was much reduced in size; its demise was soon to follow (see Plate 32). It is such deserted sites, or those that have suffered a severe decline since the early years of the nineteenth century, that make some of the most interesting and rewarding studies in the evolution of the landscape of the two counties.

SELECT BIBLIOGRAPHY

Beavington, F., 'Early market gardening in Bedfordshire', *Transactions of the Institute of British Geographers,* 37 (1965), pp. 91–100.

Beavington, F., 'The development of Market Gardening in Bedfordshire, 1799–1939', *Agricultural History Review,* 23, Part I (1975), pp. 23–47.

Britten, J. and Brayley, E. W., *The Beauties of England and Wales. Bedfordshire* (1801) and *Huntingdonshire* (1808).

Lysons, Rev. D. and S., *Magna Britannia* (1813).

Marshall, W., *Review and Abstracts of the County Reports to the Board of Agriculture from the several Agricultural Departments of England,* Vol. 4, The Midlands (first published 1815, David and Charles facsimile reprint, n.d.).

[8] H.R.O. TLR 468.

8. Communications and rural industry

The pre-railway age. The impact of the railways.

The pre-railway age

EVEN IN THE seventeenth century transport within the two counties was still cumbersome and slow. Most people set their horizons no further than the nearest market town and members of the great landed families thought twice before embarking upon a journey over any distance unless it involved travelling upon the Great North Road, as it gradually became known, or Watling Street. We know that these roads were well used by the seventeenth century, for some of the earliest stretches of turnpike came into being along them and both routes were used by the cattle drovers making for the London meat markets. But for the movement of local agricultural produce and particularly for the import of heavy, bulky goods the turnpikes were of little use; it was to the waterway of the Great Ouse that the developers of this kind of traffic were to turn.

The difficulties of the navigation of the Great Ouse above St Ives were only too well known, both physical and man made. The biggest problem concerned stretches of shallow water. Boat owners were often forced to purchase a head of water from the owners of mills upstream—millers held the water back to power their mill streams—in order to proceed (see Plate 35). But in 1617 a Middlesex man, John Gason from Finchley, obtained a patent from the Crown which enabled him to make the river navigable over a period of twenty-one years. Gason assigned his rights to a local man,

Arnold Spencer of Cople, and it was he who began the task of constructing sluices between St Ives and St Neots in order to control the flow of the water and assist boats past the many mills. For fifty years the work continued fitfully, until the rights were leased to Henry Ashley of Eynesbury who built more sluices towards Bedford, the ultimate goal of the navigation. For some time the head of navigation on the Ouse was at Great Barford, several miles downstream from the town where wharves and warehouses were constructed around the church close to the bridge across the river. Where a few years previous there had been but 'a poore Inne of 2 beds' several inns were built. Church House survives today as the former home of the navigation offices and part of the wharf can still be recognised along the old river front that runs from Bridge Cottage down to the present weir. In 1689 Bedford was at last reached by boats that had freedom of navigation all the way to the North Sea. The town soon took on the role of a regional centre for the distribution of coal; wharves were built on the south bank of the river, some of them where the County Hotel now stands, replacing the tanneries that had formerly existed.

The Ouse Navigation continued in use until the end of the nineteenth century, but little remains today of the early works of improvement. A number of the locks bear the initials C & F, named after Cullum and Franklin who were responsible for river works in the 1840s. John Franklin was a Great Barford man who had taken a share in the ownership of the Navigation Company.

The improvement of river transport on the Ouse spread to its tributary, the Ivel. As early as 1758 the Ivel was made navigable from its junction with the Ouse at Tempsford to Biggleswade, where wharves were built on either side of the parish church. In 1822 it was extended a further six miles to Shefford, an achievement only made possible by a number of canal cuts. That last part of the improved navigation of the Ivel was not very successful for within fifty years it had fallen into disuse; now it is difficult to trace the line of the artificial cuts as many parts have been filled in. Until recently the canal cut between Stanford and Shefford could still be seen, but now all that survives is a slight bump in the road that runs from Clifton to Stanford as it goes over the remains of a small canal bridge, the canal on either side having been filled in. The Ivel Navigation was wound up in 1876.

In spite of the improvements of the rivers for navigation the great phase of canal building was to by-pass rural Bedfordshire and to ignore Huntingdonshire completely. The Grand Junction Canal approached Bedfordshire's western borders; it passed through Leighton Linslade on its way from London to the Midlands and was to have some influence upon the south-western part of the county. The Duke of Bedford made use of the Grand Junction to bring in Bath stone for the building work at Woburn, and the canal was able to compete with the Ouse Navigation in the shipment of coal. In 1811, a few years after the completion of the Grand Junction, a proposal was made for linking the canal with the Ouse but in spite of receiving the support of most of the county's large landowners nothing more was heard of the scheme.

By the early nineteenth century the main roads through the counties had been improved, most of them through the action of the Turnpike Trusts. It is not known when the Great North Road, the present A1, became the more important of the two routes that left London for the North. The northbound roads rejoined at Alconbury, just beyond Huntingdon, but it is interesting to note that Speed's county map of Huntingdonshire for 1610 only marks the more easterly route, that of Ermine Street. Morden's maps of the seventeenth century show the west route only as far south as St Neots, yet as early as 1622 there had been an attempt to turnpike a stretch of that same road between Biggleswade and Baldock in Hertfordshire. Certainly by the end of the seventeenth century it had assumed a much greater importance than hitherto.

The earliest of the Turnpike Trusts to be established in the two counties dealt with parts of the A1 through Huntingdonshire, parts that have already been discussed in relation to the Bullock Road. In 1706 Watling Street between Hockcliffe and Stony Stratford in Buckinghamshire was turnpiked, followed only a few years later by its extension southwards to Dunstable. Within a few decades most of the main roads of the two counties were controlled by Turnpike Trusts, although Huntingdonshire lagged behind Bedfordshire on account of the lighter traffic and hence the lower revenue that could be expected. By 1808 the following was said of that county's roads:

> The high roads of Huntingdonshire are in general pretty good; the cross roads are but indifferent; and in the winter season many of them impassable.[1]

Other contemporary writers had little praise for the minor roads which appear to have been in a poor state apart from the district around Bedford and the area around Cardington where the roads had apparently been improved at the expense of Samuel Whitbread. Rather surprisingly, there was no public carriage road in operation between Luton and Dunstable.

With the turnpikes came the gates and the little toll houses that were once a feature of the roadside landscape all over England. Bedfordshire had over thirty toll houses, but now very few survive. The least altered can be seen on Vinegar Hill, Northill, on the old turnpike route that ran from Hitchin to join the Great North Road at Sandy. In Huntingdonshire they have practically all fallen foul of the road widening schemes that have affected every stretch of the A1 since the war. Many have been abandoned in favour of less cramped and quieter conditions. Several of the milestones

[1] Britten, J. and Brayley, E. W., op. cit.

that were erected by the Trusts can still be found, although they too have often been discarded in a ditch or hedge. Some of the more elaborate signposts have survived. The fine direction obelisk at Bell End, Brampton, now stands in the middle of a roundabout. At Alconbury Weston, where the Great North Road used to emerge from the village to climb the long hill northwards, stands the stone pillar that used to indicate the alternative routes to London. The unceasing traffic of the twentieth century now speeds by, and its position upon the central reservation must ensure that no one would dare venture to stop for a closer look!

Much of the work of the Turnpike Trusts has been superseded and only fragments survive, but the effect they had upon coaching traffic is still evident in the many fine coaching inns that were built in practically every town and village along the important routes to the north and north-west. Coaches plied between the towns on a regular basis and even a place like Bedford, small though it was in the early part of the nineteenth century, had a considerable traffic throughout the week. Pigot's Commercial Directory for 1824 lists eight different coach companies serving the town during the week, some of them making several trips. Coach routes stretched out to London, Leeds, Cambridge and Oxford, with links more direct than those offered by the present system of public transport!

Along the Great North Road and Watling Street the great coaching inns grew up. Dunstable revived in the eighteenth century as a result of the increase of passing traffic, lifting it from a long period of decline into which it had fallen since the extinction of the priory. There were over twenty inns lining the four main streets of the compact little town. Modern redevelopment has not been kind to the eighteenth-century townscape of Dunstable; practically nothing remains today apart from the occasional archway of an inn that formerly allowed the coaches access to the rear courtyard. Biggleswade and St Neots have fared rather better, although even there better examples remain of nineteenth-century architecture rather than the more graceful building of the earlier period. Huntingdon still has the George Hotel with part of a seventeenth-century courtyard and one range of the external gallery that was once a common feature of so many of the roadside inns.

In the villages, where the pressures for redevelopment have not been felt, some of the best examples of coaching inns survive. Buckden has two of them. The Lion certainly goes back to the days before the road was of any importance for it was used in the fifteenth century as an outer guest house to the bishop's palace. The high archway that marks the entrance to the rear courtyard can still be recognised, although it is now blocked up. On the other side of the road stands the tall, red-brick façade of the George, built in the plain style of the mid-eighteenth century when the coach trade was at its peak. Not all of the structure is used as an hotel today, part being given up to shop premises. Another inn that was rebuilt to cope with the demands of the coach trade lies just a few miles further north up the Great North Road, the Bell at Stilton. Built in 1642 upon the site of an older inn, it is now in a forlorn state, empty and semi-derelict. At the time of writing the future of the Bell remains uncertain, yet it was perhaps the most famous of all the coaching inns south of Stamford for it was here that the famous Stilton cheese was made and sold to the passing travellers in the early years of the eighteenth century. Exactly when or for what reason the production of the cheese moved to Leicestershire remains a matter for debate but it was not that which killed off the trade of the Bell; rather the coming of the motor age and the by-passing of the little settlement so that hardly anyone ventures to stop or even to turn off the main road to view this once thriving place. One may only hope that the suggestions for turning the Bell into a fashionable restaurant will revive its ancient tradition (Plate 33).

The Haycock at Wansford has been more successful, partly because it can still be seen from the by-pass (the last stretch of dual carriageway of the A1 to be completed in the two counties). It too had been built in the middle of the seventeenth century, in 1662, but apparently as a new posting station for the long distance coaches. Its architectural style, and the mellow Jurassic stone of which it is constructed, again recall a scene that is more familiar over the border in Northamptonshire than in the rest of Huntingdonshire.

The inns on the main roads were not only used by the passing coach traffic but also acted as an important meeting place for those concerned with the enclosure of the open fields. Even though the parish concerned might lie some distance from the road, it often happened that no inn existed within the village. The commissioners therefore chose to conduct their business at one of the coaching inns, no doubt well supported with ample dinners at the expense of the parish. Eleven years of deliberation passed before the enclosure of Glatton with Holme, and the meetings took place alternatively at the Bell and Angel inns in Stilton, because no suitable accommodation was at hand within the two villages.

The impact of the railways

When the first railway appeared on the western border of Bedfordshire with the opening of a station at Leighton Linslade on the London to Birmingham line in 1838, few of the coach owners on the turnpikes or the coal hauliers on the Ouse could have realised how rapidly their trade would decline in the face of very stiff competition. At first, coach companies benefited from the new station for it provided them with the opportunity of new services to the nearby towns. In a similar way, when the Eastern Counties line opened from London to Cambridge in 1845 coaches ran connecting services from St Neots and Huntingdon to Cambridge. When the same company opened a branch line to Hertford two years later a coach service started to Eaton Socon, providing a quicker route to London than the coach journey down the Great North Road. It was not until 1850, with the opening of the London to York line, that the Great North Road received its first direct challenge from the railway. Even then the cross-country routes through Huntingdonshire were to remain unaffected for several decades longer. The Great Northern line was comparatively easy to construct across the rolling lowlands of Bedfordshire and Huntingdonshire but the crossing of the peat lands of Sawtry Fen and between Holme and Yaxley presented a greater obstacle. The line runs on the top of a high embankment, a feat of engineering skill that employed many thousands in its manual construction and involved the use of thousands of tons of earth.

The Eastern Region's main line to the north is the only one that now survives in Huntingdonshire for the branch line across the Fens to Ramsey and Warboys has been closed, as have the railways that connected Huntingdon with Kettering and St Ives and Cambridge. Even at their peak, at the end of the last century, these lines failed to serve large areas of Huntingdonshire and those places within reach of the railways cannot have been very profitable. The economic potential of the rural parts of Huntingdonshire could not have been very high at the time when the railway map was completed for the countryside had been losing population for several decades and the location of the few rural stations, at some considerable distance from town or village, can have hardly encouraged their use. Kimbolton's station, for example, was over two miles away and Brampton's more than a mile. The lines themselves are now difficult to find in places; not only has the track been removed but often the land has been returned to agricultural use. In the Fens in particular, where there are no awkward cuttings or embankments and land is at a premium, the line of the former permanent way can no longer be traced on the ground along much of the length of the branch from Ramsey to Holme.

Bedfordshire had more branch lines than Huntingdonshire and a better coverage of the whole country was provided. Bedford became the centre of a network of local and national lines. In the 1840s a group of the town's businessmen had formed the Bedford Railway Company with the intention of providing a link with the London to Birmingham line at Bletchley in Buckinghamshire. Their new line was opened in 1846 and proved to be of some benefit to the town but it was of even greater importance in opening up the brick-making area to the south. Within twenty-five years six lines radiated from Bedford. The first station was built on the south side of the town to the south of the River Ouse, at St Johns. By 1857 the river had been bridged by the Leicester to Hitchin line and a new station built on the western edge of the town, the present Midland Station. In 1868 that line was extended to provide a direct link to St Pancras in London. The Midland Railway Company was able to withdraw from the previous unsatisfactory arrangements whereby they had shared the line of the Great Northern south from Hitchin.

Dunstable and Luton achieved stations at an early stage in railway development, although Dunstable initially gained at Luton's expense. In 1848 a branch line had been proposed from Luton to Leighton Buzzard with the prospect of links with the first main line in the region, the London to Birmingham. But Luton objected to the proposed route across the town's common pasture of Great Moor; the line was therefore terminated instead at Dunstable. It was another ten years before this branch line was continued eastwards and another twenty years elapsed before the peace of the Great Moor was finally shattered when the new St Pancras line cut diagonally across the common land, part of which was sold off for housing development.

The effect of the railways upon the two counties cannot be easily disentangled from new industrial developments, especially within the towns. They certainly killed off the road and river trade. On the Saturday following the opening of the Bedford to Bletchley line in 1846 the Bedford Times coach left Bedford for the last time. Toll receipts from the various gates along the turnpikes were halved within a matter of a few years of direct competition from the railways. Only the turnpike from Bedford to Kimbolton was to hold its own for any length of time because there was no direct rail link. On the River Ouse the coal traffic—which had dominated the Navigation Company's receipts since the river had been made navigable up to Bedford—had already suffered from the competition provided by the Grand Junction Canal in south-west Bedfordshire, but now trade collapsed and by the end of the century steps were being taken to sell off the rights that had once proved so profitable.

The effect of the railways upon the towns was not always favourable, particularly where one town was fortunate in being placed upon a main line route while its rival had only a branch line. Cambridge was better served in that respect than St Ives, although the latter had always had the advantage in terms of river transport. The small agricultural towns of the two counties, within which one might include both Bedford and Huntingdon in the middle of the nineteenth century, do not exhibit any marked acceleration in their rates of growth following the introduction of a railway station and speedier access not only to other parts of the county but also to London—the largest of the markets for agricultural produce. Sandy is the one exception. Bedford, for example, although it became the route centre of a half-dozen lines shows very little growth at all in the first thirty years after the coming of the railways. Luton was the only place to grow rapidly and much of that can be attributed to the development of the straw hat industry rather than to the railway, for its population had already risen from 2,986 in

1821 to 10,648 in 1851, the latter date some seven years before the first railway reached the town. Indeed, the compilers of the 1851 Census Returns commented that the town was the largest in the country that had neither railway nor navigable river.

The infrequent spacing of stations and halts suggests that the railways gained very little traffic from the countryside of the two counties. Only the market gardening around Sandy depended upon good communications with London, and the arrival of the Great Northern Line not only enabled growers to reach that city far more rapidly but also made available large quantities of horse manure from London's stables. This was put to good use in expanding the market garden acreage, particularly on to the infertile Lower Greensand west and east of Sandy. By the end of the century this intensive, specialised form of agriculture had spread as far west as Ampthill where it was prevented from further expansion by the opposition of the Russells, owners of the Ampthill Estate, to such development. Over seven thousand acres were then in use for market gardening and by 1905 goods trains left Biggleswade Station for London four times a week in the busy season loaded with vegetables.[2] So essential was the railway considered for Sandy's development that in 1857 Captain William Peel, son of the more famous Sir Robert Peel, paid for the construction of a four-mile link from Potton to the Great Northern Line at Sandy. The line was said to be for the 'use of London manure by his tenants . . . and taking thence passengers, garden produce etc.' Although there is little contemporary evidence of an immediate impact of this improvement in transport, there is little doubt that the railway contributed to the disappearance of heathland at Sandy, Gamlingay (Cambridgeshire) and Potton in the last quarter of the century when they were converted to market gardens. The names of the former heaths can still be found on the maps of the Ordnance

[2] Beavington, F., op. cit. (1975).

Survey, together with Warren Farm in Sandy (alongside Peel's railway line) but the picture is now one of intense cultivation in small, enclosed fields. The line later extended eastwards to Cambridge, but it has been closed since the late 1960s and all the vegetables are sent to market by road, just as they were until the railway came one hundred and twenty years ago.

The railways prompted the expansion of one rural enterprise, the making of bricks. Clay-pits and small brick kilns were a common sight in the early nineteenth-century landscape of the two counties and a concentration of brick-making was already evident around the edge of the Fens and in central Bedfordshire. The railways gave a distinct advantage to certain places and the scale of enterprises increased. New sites emerged alongside or close to the railways. Only two years after the completion of the Great Northern line through eastern Bedfordshire in 1850 a large brickworks was set up beside the railway at Arlesley. The kilns produced the creamy yellow bricks that are so often encountered in fen-edge villages. They also characterise the long street village of Arlesley itself. The late-nineteenth-century cottages and houses stretch for over a mile south from the little village centre with its former agricultural cottages grouped around the open space by the church. Further north on the same line, just south of the village of Fletton, new pits were opened on either side of the track. Today the railway rides a precarious embankment above huge pits that cover hundreds of acres. Although the reclamation of disused pits is now under way, this district still has the greatest concentration of derelict land in eastern England south of the Humber. Almost as large an area exists in central Bedfordshire centred on the brickworks 'village' of Stewartby and the ravaged parish of Wootton. In Wootton some of the biggest changes came with the opening of the Bedford to Bletchley line in 1846. By the end of the century new clay-workings had been opened in an area already pocked by small pits and kilns over the previous two centuries. In 1894 the Luton firm of B. J. H. Forder opened a brickworks at Westoning, quite close to Harlington Station, and several years later embarked upon much larger schemes at Elstow and Wootton Pillinge, the latter one of Wootton's hamlets. The Elstow works are now derelict and the pit at Westoning is scarcely recognisable as a former brick pit, but the Wootton Pillinge works stands amid one of the largest brickmaking complexes in Europe. Again, most of the bricks are now distributed by road but quite a number of the brickworks still have their sidings, and goods trains loaded with bricks are a common sight (see Plate 34).

During the nineteenth century the brick companies made little attempt to supply accommodation for their workers and so the adjacent villages expanded with the addition of cottages for workers in the brickfields. Growth was very rapid for some settlements, particularly over the period 1831–81, the very time that other remote rural parishes were experiencing contraction. It is probable that the brickworks encouraged quite a number of rural labourers to abandon the land for jobs in the brickfields. While some of the villages showed a two or three-fold increase over the fifty-year period, the figures below reveal that Fletton's increase was almost ten-fold.

Population change in Brick Making Parishes 1831–81

	1831	*1881*
Arlesley	688	1908
Wootton	1051	1302
Fletton	189	1841
Farcet	536	710

By the close of the nineteenth century the railways had ousted road and river traffic from much of the two counties. The Ouse and Ivel Navigations fell into disuse and all the

Turnpike Trusts had collapsed by the last quarter of the century. Places that were formerly well served by road or river declined rapidly if they lay outside the range of a railway station. Many of the roadside inns never recovered; others received a new life when they were rediscovered by motorists and cyclists. Often this recovery was brief if the construction of a by-pass diverted the new travellers. But along the rivers trade never revived and warehouses have been demolished or turned to other purposes. Even the mills that had once been such a problem for the boat owners have been superseded by larger and more modern structures in the towns and seaports. At least the skeletons of many of the fine eighteenth- and nineteenth-century mills survive (see Plate 35), even if their water wheels and working machinery have invariably gone.

SELECT BIBLIOGRAPHY

Cockman, F. G., 'The Railway Age in Bedfordshire', *Bedfordshire Historical Record Society*, 53 (1974).

Emmison, F. G., 'Turnpike Roads and Toll Gates in Bedfordshire', *Bedfordshire Historical Record Society*, 18 (1936).

Summers, D., *The Great Ouse* (1973).

V.C.H. *Bedfordshire*, Vol. II (1908).

V.C.H. *Huntingdonshire*, Vol. II (1932).

9. The landscape of towns

The small market towns. Huntingdon and Godmanchester. Luton and Bedford.

The small market towns

WE HAVE ALREADY discussed the origin and early growth of the small market towns that are a prominent feature of the two counties, particularly those that were newly established in the Middle Ages. Markets sometimes grew in established villages and the morphology of the settlement was modified to encompass a market place. This happened at Toddington in Bedfordshire, where a late-sixteenth-century map of the manor shows the centre of the village occupied by a large market place, free of the encroachments that can now be seen on the grass-covered space. Encroachment upon the market place is a common theme that repeats itself in most of the former market towns and villages. For instance, Ramsey's medieval market place is now obscured by buildings that lie between the High Street and Little Whyte, although the great width of Great Whyte, running at right angles to the High Street, could easily be mistaken for the site of the market. But it derives its shape from the canal that formerly ran down its centre, a reminder of the time when remote Ramsey relied upon the fenland waterways for its contact and trade with the outside world. We do not know the full extent of Luton's market, but it is now represented by a tiny triangle—Market Hill—which is little more than a broadening of the road within a one-way traffic scheme. Some of the other medieval market towns have fared better and open spaces still dominate the plans of

St Ives, St Neots, Kimbolton, Leighton Buzzard and Biggleswade.

By the end of the eighteenth century many of the markets had declined. Lysons commented on Toddington that it was in decline although 'a century ago this town had one of the most considerable markets in the county'.[1] In its latter years the market came to depend greatly upon the sale of straw plait and this was to prove its downfall in the middle of the nineteenth century when trade collapsed in the face of foreign competition. The timbered market house that stood upon the market-place when the manor was surveyed and mapped in 1581 was already disused by 1800. At Harrold the little green, formerly the market place, still survives with its attractive open market hall, built in the early part of the eighteenth century when the town was still important for the sale of pillow lace, a cottage industry of north Bedfordshire and Northamptonshire (see Plate 36). It too had declined by the beginning of the following century for Lysons' comment was that it was only used each week by one or two butchers and the trade in pillow lace appears to have died altogether.

Several of the market towns were severely damaged by fire during the seventeenth and eighteenth centuries and this accounts for their present Georgian and Victorian frontages. One cannot assume that an extensive rebuilding in the styles of the eighteenth and nineteenth century betoken an increased prosperity in the markets of that period. St Ives, for example, was damaged by fire in 1689 when '122 messuages, dwellings etc.' were destroyed, most of them in the market place.[2] Biggleswade suffered a similar holocaust in 1785 when a hundred and eighty-five buildings were lost. The rebuilding at Biggleswade was not to a very high standard, a reflection of the decline of its market function—something which the Ivel Navigation failed to reverse. Professor

[1] Lysons, Rev. D. and S., *Magna Britannia* (1813).
[2] Britten, J. and Brayley, W., op. cit. (1808).

Pevsner has described it as a town of little architectural merit and visually disappointing. Potton and Ramsey also had serious fires during the eighteenth century, although it is unlikely that either suffered a great loss as far as buildings of high architectural merit were concerned for both had relied upon serving an area dominated by small farmers and smallholders. Potton had a fine new shambles in 1800, but that has now been replaced by a neo-Georgian clock tower, built in 1956. In contrast, the majority of attractive red brick houses in the centre of Woburn date from a rebuilding after a fire in 1724. A new butchers' shambles was built in 1737 in a building whose upper storey also served for the corn market; in 1830 that was replaced by the present market house.

Huntingdon and Godmanchester

These two towns, facing each other across the Ouse but separated by a quarter-mile stretch of meadow, had long been rivals, although Godmanchester was only a large village throughout the Middle Ages at a time when Huntingdon ranked among the most important towns of eastern England. The latter was said to have had sixteen medieval churches, together with three monasteries and three hospitals, while Godmanchester was served by only its parish church. Yet the village was one of the largest agricultural settlements in Huntingdonshire and when Huntingdon's fortunes began to decline in the sixteenth century Godmanchester was to grow in importance so as to rival the ancient borough.

By the early sixteenth century Huntingdon's sixteen churches had been reduced to four, and after the Civil War only two were left standing. Edmund Gibson, writing the additions to Camden's Britannia, observed that 'the zeal of the late times only left two'. Those two still stand; All Saints by the Market Place, and St Mary further down the High

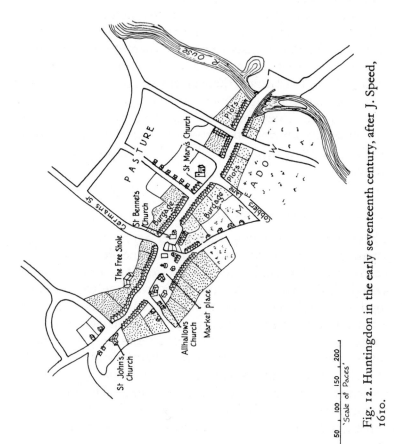

Fig. 12. Huntingdon in the early seventeenth century, after J. Speed, 1610.

Street towards the River Ouse. Of the others, only the churchyard of St John Baptist remains, a short distance north of the market.

Huntingdon's importance waned until the borough received a temporary boost from the improvement of the river navigation and the growth of the coach trade. Although there have been many irreparable losses to twentieth-century redevelopment in the town, Huntingdon still presents a Georgian face in places, reflecting one of its periods of prosperity. The red brick Town Hall on the Market Place dates from 1745 and traces of some of the eighteenth-century inns around the centre can still be seen. The Falcon remains and the upper floors of the Fountain, long the rival of the George which was mentioned in the last chapter, can be seen above the modern frontage of Woolworths.

Huntingdon's town plan was very simple and appears to have changed little from the early years of the seventeenth century when Speed included it on his county map. Running north from the late medieval bridge across the Ouse is the High Street, with the market place lying along it and a number of narrow lanes running back from the street frontage (see Fig. 12). The market place appears to have been encroached upon even in Speed's day, but it was certainly larger in the seventeenth century than today. The present street plan gives the impression of an oval-shaped town—one which might have had a medieval wall. But this is deceptive, for an inner ring road, a very recent construction which runs on its south and west over former meadows has given to Huntingdon its intriguing shape. New developments have not treated what is left of the medieval core very kindly. The High Street is dominated by modern shop frontages that can be found in countless other high streets across the country and the chain stores can be criticised here for their lack of sympathy with the Georgian façades that once dominated the townscape; such styles are seen better away from the shops. Behind the shops the destruction is far worse for the former long, narrow burgage plots of the ancient borough are no more and the narrow lanes and alleys that accompanied them have also been obliterated in the desire to create large car parks and a small shopping precinct, the latter a most undistinguished piece of building. One wonders how much future generations will look back with dismay at this typical example of mediocre redevelopment that has ruined many of our small towns. When the aesthetic bill of reckoning for the twentieth century comes to be calculated our property developers will have much to answer for in the destruction of such towns.

As Huntingdon has become the main shopping centre for the area, Godmanchester has managed to retain far more of its historic buildings. Now that the east coast traffic has been removed through the opening of a by-pass the quiet little town is once more a joy to explore. The once royal manor developed within the confines of the former Roman town and although it did not retain its urban status it enjoyed an unusual privilege, confirmed by King John in 1212, whereby its inhabitants were known as free tenants and were entitled to a degree of self government, something normally only reserved to those towns where a charter had been granted. Unlike the burgesses of Huntingdon, they were not allowed to sell or give away their land, although that privilege was to come in the seventeenth century when Godmanchester acquired its own charter. By then the street plan was well established and was not to be altered by the growth of the market; the little borough is therefore unusual in not having a central market place or any evidence of burgage plots. Instead the centre grew in a haphazard way, with houses and small gardens scattered along paths and lanes within the enclosing roads that we have already recognised as encompassing the old Roman town. Even today one can drive around the centre but it is with difficulty that one can find a route that goes through it.

Godmanchester's growing importance in the seventeenth

and eighteenth centuries can be seen in the considerable number of buildings surviving from that date. Some belonged to merchants but the majority were the houses of yeoman farmers. The older buildings are massive timber-framed structures but later ones, such as Farm Hall on the western outskirts of the town, were normally built of brick. Although the river became an important focal point, with boats tying up along the Causeway, the survival of the town's West and East Side commons bears witness to the strength of the farming tradition down to the present day. Yet how many agricultural communities could boast of a grammar school in the sixteenth century. Its little red brick Queen Elizabeth Grammar School is still to be seen at the northern end of the Causeway.

Luton and Bedford

Of all the towns in the two counties Luton's growth since 1800 has been the most impressive. Indeed, apart from a number of seaside towns, Luton has grown faster than almost any other urban community in southern England. In 1800 Luton was only a small town; its prosperity depended upon a local market and a circle of ancillary hamlets. Certainly it was less important than Huntingdon, but as the latter borough was settling into a decline Luton soon came to surpass it in size and importance. Even in 1821 its population was only 2,986 (excluding the hamlets), half the size of Bedford. Within twenty years Luton rose to 5,827 and by 1861 the total surpassed 15,000. The 1891 Census shows that Luton had outstripped Bedford and it has continued through the twentieth century as the largest town of the two counties. Its 1971 total was 161,405, more than double that of the county town.

Luton's population history suggests that there is little to see there from the centuries before 1800. There are huge areas of mid-Victorian, Edwardian and inter-war growth, not to mention the ever-growing sprawl of post-war estates, all a reflection of the rapid industrial expansion of the town in recent decades. Of the pre-industrial town very little is visible apart from the retention of fragments of the original street pattern. The compact centre was bounded by George Street, Park Street and the North Mill (Mill Street). At the southern end of George Street was Market Hill, formerly known by the more ancient name for a market, Chipping Hill. The River Lea formed the original eastern boundary of Luton, but as the stream now runs in culverts it is no longer traceable on the ground. North of the town centre lay two tracts of common pasture, Great and Little Moor, lying on either side of the Old Bedford Road.

The main impetus to Luton's growth in the early nineteenth century came from the development of the straw hat industry. Before 1800 most hat manufacturers were located in London, where firms imported most of their materials from abroad and worked only for a restricted quality market. During the long years of war with France at the turn of the eighteenth century foreign supplies became scarce and the demands of the London hatters turned to local supplies of straw plait. The best plait was obtained from the chalklands of north Hertfordshire and southern Bedfordshire and although the reason for this locational preference is not altogether clear, it is noted that contemporary writers stressed the importance of chalkland for good quality straw. The use of local straw plait by the London hatters was only temporary but it may well have been sufficient to give a boost to the development of hat-making in Luton, the small prosperous Bedfordshire town being better placed than any others to benefit from the availability of good quality straw plait. Yet it was Dunstable that was to benefit first, for manufacturers were still aiming at an expensive market and there was a ready outlet there in the many coaches that travelled through on the London to Chester road. When the supplies of foreign material returned, the manufacturers of straw plait were forced to improve the quality of their products and to devise means of producing straw hats cheaply. In 1826 Thomas Waller patented the Tuscan Straw Bonnet and his brother set up a warehouse in Luton where he purchased hats for resale over the whole of the country. By the 1840s several London firms had moved part of their enterprise to Luton, the first being that of the Vyse family. The town grew rapidly as a centre for straw hat manufacture, opening up a new market among the masses. It is clear, therefore, that the railway had little to do with the initial growth of Luton as an industrial centre. The extension of the railway from Dunstable to Luton did not happen until 1858, by which times Luton had already achieved supremacy over the former with some forty hat manufacturers in the town. Sixty years later hat-making dominated the town. There were over four hundred firms and 11,000 employees.

The growth of the industry attracted labour into Luton from the surrounding villages, particularly when the making of straw plait that had nurtured the industry collapsed in the second half of the century as a result of the importation of great quantities of cheap plait from the Far East. The cottage industry had been largely in the hands of women and children—early schools appear to have devoted considerable attention to it—and it was female labour that was most in demand by the hat industry. Many plait makers moved to Luton and turned their hands to bonnet and hat-making instead.

The majority of the firms at the end of the nineteenth century were very small. Their workshops formed part of the rows of terraced houses that sprang up on the outskirts of the market town. Many of these two-storeyed workshops still survive, distinguished by their large windows that provided enough light for those who worked in the two big rooms. The ground floor room was used for the heavier work of blocking and stiffening of the plait, a task in which men were usually employed. In the upper room women were engaged in sewing (see Plate 37). Behind the houses and workshops you find a narrow lane, a service road for carts that supplied these cottage factories. Some terraces still retain a wide archway entrance that gave access to carts from the service road.

The earliest expansion beyond the original nucleus of Luton came to the south-west, between Castle Street and Dallow Road, as well as in the adjacent area of New Town. In the latter the first conveyance was concerned with a property in New Town Street in 1834. Growth was soon apparent to the north of the railway stations, spreading up the hill towards High Town. Although both these areas have undergone considerable transformation in recent years, with the demolition of many of the poor terraces and their replacement with flats and newly aligned roads, it is still possible to recognise a number of the streets where the hat industry once flourished. At the time of writing, several terraces with their rear passages still intact remain on the northern side of High Town Road, close to Peoples Park. Frederick Street and Frederick Street Passage are the best survivors in Luton of the mixture of industry and private homes that used to characterise so much of the town in the Victorian era. How much longer, one wonders, will they be allowed to survive? Will the few hat manufacturers that can still be found in Luton be there in ten years' time, given the great decline in hat wearing that has been a feature of post-war Britain? To the south of High Town Road the old industrial and residential landscape has already gone; today 'planner's blight' has left the area empty, a few distributive trades scattered amongst grass-covered car parks and streets that no longer have any houses.

The old centre of Luton was also penetrated by the hat trade for that was where the larger firms established themselves. After the coming of the railway, George Street, which had been the principal shopping street, was taken over by the hat manufacturers and the late-nineteenth-century scene was one of bustle and activity as carts took hats from small warehouses along the street to the railway station. The shopping centre shifted to Wellington Street, at right angles to the former axis. Only in the last few decades has the focus of shopping moved back into George Street, but now it is being challenged by the new covered Arndale Centre that lies alongside. This new shopping complex has swept away an area of nineteenth-century buildings, where hat firms, warehouses, churches, schools and residential property were inter-mixed along a muddle of streets, together with the former Plait Halls, the straw plait market. A few remnants of that landscape can still be seen between the Arndale Centre and the railway station (Luton Midland Road), of which the most prominent is the huge hat warehouse that stood alongside the former Bute Street Station. The station, the first to be built in Luton when the line arrived from Dunstable in 1858, has been demolished and the land now serves as a British Rail car park for nearby Midland Road Station.

The railways not only gave further impetus to Luton's industrial growth, but also provided the reason for the destruction of the Great Moor. The new line from Bedford to London, opened in 1868, crossed the Moor. The trustees sought to sell off part of the old common grazing land at the same time. John Crawley of Stockwood Park, prominent businessman and landowner, made a shrewd move in acquiring the part of the Great Moor to the south of the railway line in return for land at High Town. The thirteen acres of level ground that he acquired from the Common provided attractive sites for speculative building. They lay close to the town-centre, and were more than ample compensation for the twenty acres of steeply sloping ground acquired by the trustees. Part of the trustees' new ground can still be seen in the form of the open spaces of Pope's Meadow and Peoples Park, their steep slopes offering good views over much of the town centre, while the Great Moor lies under houses; here Crawley Road, Francis Street and Moor Street were constructed by John Crawley. Five acres of the Great Moor were set aside as grazing land. It lay north of the railway, bounded on the east by the New Bedford Road, and it can still be recognised as one of Luton's small parks.

In spite of Luton's rapid growth during the nineteenth century the neighbouring hamlets remained separate from the built-up area until they were swallowed up in the expansion of the inter-war and post-war years. In 1894, a time of local government reorganisation, they were even given separate civil status as Luton Rural, a status of separation that they had not enjoyed for centuries. But administrative independence was short lived for in the inter-war period Leagrave, Limsbury and Stopsley were reabsorbed and the remainder, excluding West Hyde, are now wholly or partially included in Luton, the town's control having returned, albeit in a different form, to that of the earlier royal manor.

The industrial make-up of Luton has changed completely in the twentieth century from hat-making to engineering. The hat trade reached its peak even before the First World War and as early as 1900 it was recognised that new industries were essential for continued growth. The forward-looking Town Corporation and the town's Chamber of Commerce co-operated to produce a booklet, aimed at attracting alternative industry to the town. 'Luton as an Industrial Centre' advertised the town's advantages, its abundant cheap land, skilled labour force and the availability of sites adjacent to the railway. As the hat industry employed so many women, the booklet was even able to advertise the advantage of being able to employ men at low rates as female members of the family were already in employment. Some of the land for industrial development belonged to the Luton Land Company, a syndicate that had foreseen the direction in which the town would grow and which had purchased land accordingly. Much of the Luton Land Company's property had been purchased from or exchanged with the Crawleys, a family so prominent in the town's early development. One can understand better the motives of the town's official bodies when it is realised that many of the syndicate members were also members of the Town Council or the Chamber of Commerce!

The first industries attracted to Luton in the early years of this century were still associated with the hat industry. In 1903 the British Gelatine Works opened, for example, as a company supplying gelatine for the stiffening of straw hats. But then in 1905 came a new departure with the establishment of the Vauxhall and West Hydraulic Engineering Company, which two years later set up a subsidiary company, Vauxhall Motors, the vehicle manufacturer which has come to dominate the town's employment and to create a major industrial landscape in the south-east of the town. In the midst of the vast Vauxhall plant the original frontage of the 1907 factory is retained. In 1910 the Swedish firm of Skefco arrived in the town to manufacture ball-bearings (see Plate 38); together with the older engineering firm of Hayward Tyler (producing hydraulic machinery and pumps) these three firms changed the emphasis of Luton's manufacturing from hat making to light engineering. Each of the new industries chose a location alongside the railway. Then in 1927 the firm of Electrolux was established, on the site of a former aeroplane works at Leagrave, on the western side of the town. Unlike the others, Electrolux saw no great need to be alongside the railway. Since then Luton's new factories have shunned the railway in preference for industrial estates that have easy access to the main roads and today the most important link with the Midlands and the North, the M1 motorway.

The industrial growth on the western side of Luton invariably spilled over into nearby Dunstable. It too had tried to encourage industry at the beginning of the century and although its expansion has not been able to match that of Luton it nevertheless rose from a population of fewer than 5,000 in 1891 to over 25,000 by 1961. Dunstable and Luton now merge into each other and the population of the two towns accounts for more than forty per cent of the total population of Bedfordshire.

Luton's rapid growth since 1800, and particularly since 1850, has been in two directions only, north and west of the old centre. Development to the south and east has been deterred by the occurrence of steep slopes, for the small town lay in a gap of the Chalk escarpment, and by the existence of two large estates, Stockwood Park and Luton Hoo. What little room there was for development has been taken up by the Vauxhall Motors plant close to the railway. It is interesting to reflect that although the Crawleys were influential in encouraging the rapid growth of Luton and were quite prepared to make capital from it, they were not prepared to see the town encroach southwards towards their house and landscaped park. It is noticeable that the housing that now fringes the park (today a public park and a municipal golf course) belongs to the inter-war period and no earlier. Stockwood Park's house, built in 1740, is unfortunately no more, the victim of a vacillating local authority which purchased the estate. The house fell into ruins and had to be demolished in 1964. Luton Hoo remains the one redeeming feature of Luton's ugly environs, its landscaped grounds of 1,500 acres contained by a long brick wall. Yet if that park had not been there one wonders how rapidly those acres would have been consumed by the expanding town? Twentieth-century Luton might well have had a completely different shape. Before the meteoric rise of Luton, Bedford was for long the most important town in the county. Although it now ranks as the second largest town, Bedford still lacks the atmosphere of an industrial town despite its population of some 80,000. The chief reason lies in its continued role as centre of services and local government.

For more than 900 years the King's Ditch acted as an effective barrier to the southward expansion of Bedford. The first railway station, St John's, was built just outside the Ditch. North of the River Ouse, the Bedford of 1820 was little different from that of 1610, with houses reaching only as far as St Peters Green. Some growth had begun along Bromham Road and Dame Alice Street (then Harpur Street), where groups of houses and almshouses had been built to replace those destroyed by fire in the St Loyes area. The most important feature of the nineteenth-century town was the market place that provided a centre of trade for farmers from many miles around. In appearance, the market place was less open at the beginning of the nineteenth century than it is today. Then it had been encroached upon by permanent market stalls and the Guildhall. It was set amidst a congested area of narrow alleys. Immediately north of the church of St Pauls was the town slaughter house—the focus of an insanitary, odious quarter. So much so, in fact, that the town cleared away eighty-two buildings from around the church in 1810, from Stonehouse Lane, High Street, Butcher Row, Church Alley, Fish Market and Vines Corner. This early nineteenth-century clearance restored the character of an open space on the north side of the bridgehead that had formerly belonged to the market place.

By 1841 Bedford's population had grown to over 9,000, but still scarcely any industries had taken root and it was another five years before the railway was to arrive. Some of the growth in mid-century can certainly be attributed to the migration of farm labourers from the parishes of central Bedfordshire, an influx of the rural poor who were seeking better opportunities elsewhere and the hope of more stable employment. What employment there was could not be divorced from the countryside either, for in 1864 commercial directories list nine maltsters in the town, and most of the early expansion was in the traditional trades of a market town. But in 1859 there came a major new source of employment in the agricultural engineering works of John Howard, the Britannia Works on the south side of the river, adjacent to the railway. The factory also had a wharf on the river, by which quantities of pig iron were transported in the early years of the works. The fame of John Howard's Britannia Works rests on the Champion Plough that found a world-wide export market. Although the factory site is now owned by a Swiss firm and turned to other purposes the elaborate factory gate, with its clock, and some of the original machine sheds and offices can still be recognised on the Kempston Road.

By the end of the century Bedford's population had reached 30,000, but its slow and modest growth, when compared with Luton, had done much to preserve the elegance of much of its centre. Like several other provincial county towns Bedford was fortunate that it became an early centre of education, the result largely of the benevolence of William Harpur and the Harpur Trust. Harpur, a local man, had risen to be Master of the Merchant Taylors Company and Lord Mayor of London in the middle of the sixteenth century. In 1564 he had purchased land in Holborn, then a village some distance from London's walls, and given it to Bedford as an endowment for a school. By the middle of the eighteenth century the property was of considerable value, caught up in London's West End expansion, and a trust was set up in 1746 to administer the funds from a greatly increased estate. As a result, the Trust was able to establish a number of schools in the town and some of their graceful buildings still remain there today. Behind St Pauls Church stands the small grammar school of the mid-eighteenth century, later to become the Town Hall, while close by is the façade of the Harpur Modern School, its Tudor castellated style begun by Wing in the 1820s as the successor to the cramped buildings on its left hand side. The school was completed in 1834 by Blore, Wing having died in 1826. Opposite stands the Harpur Suite, with its Greek Doric front (yet only of 1834), originally founded as the Literary and Scientific Institution.

Elsewhere in Bedford, away from the modern shop fronts of the town's centre, large Victorian houses abound, especially along the Embankment, a broad esplanade that fronts the river below the bridge. Beside the bridge stands the late Georgian Swan Hotel, with graceful bow windows to the first floor and the building cased in stone. Another element of Bedford's landscape is the large number of eighteenth- and nineteenth-century non-conformist chapels. Although the town was not always tolerant towards early non-conformists—after all John Bunyan was imprisoned at Bedford —there were other times when it became the centre for a number of sects. The original Old Meeting House of which Bunyan was minister no longer stands, but its successor (1850) survives as a thriving place of worship in the town. Not so the New Meeting House, almost next door but now disused. The present building is of the same age as the Old Meeting House but it succeeded a church built in the 1770s when a split from the Old Meeting occurred. One of the main supporters of the New Meeting was John Howard, the prison reformer. On the outer edge of the eighteenth- century town a group of Moravians established a community, with a church and houses for single brethren and sisters, close to St Peters Green. They opened a new church in 1865, with dwelling houses alongside, which can still be seen in St Peters Street.

Only in this century has Bedford attracted a number of new engineering firms. Its population has doubled since 1901, but over the same period Luton has grown four-fold. In recent years Bedford has continued to expand at a rapid pace, partly as a result of the settlement of several immigrant groups—Poles, Italians and Asians. Italians now account for ten per cent of Bedford's population, the result of the attraction of Italian male workers into the Bedfordshire brick industry in the 1950s when the post-war boom produced a severe shortage of labour. The London Brick Company sent a recruiting team to Naples, in the heart of poverty stricken Southern Italy, and succeeded in attracting many workers. At first, they were accommodated in hostels at the various works but later, when the rest of their families had arrived, many moved to Bedford, establishing a quarter among the late Victorian terraces to the south and west of the town centre. Today this part of Bedford is gay with the brightly coloured houses and the pot plants so beloved of these former agricultural workers, streets whose continental appearance would no doubt have shocked the Victorians who first dwelt in them.

SELECT BIBLIOGRAPHY

Austin, W., *History of Luton and its Hamlets* (1928, 2 volumes).

Baker, D. and Hassall, J., 'Bedford: Aspects of Town Origins and Development', *Beds. Arch. Jnl.,* 9 (1974), pp. 75–94.

Carmell, H. A., Booth, T. and Tibbutt, H. G., *A Kempston History* (1966).

Dyer, J. and Dony, J., *The Story of Luton* (1975, 3rd Ed.).

King, R., 'Bedford: the Italian connection', *Geographical Magazine,* XLIX, No. 7 (1977), pp. 442–449.

Law, C. M., 'Luton and the Hat Industry', *The East Midland Geographer,* 4, Part 6 (1968), pp. 329–341.

Lysons, Rev. D. and S., *Magna Britannia* (1813).

Pevsner, N., *The Buildings of England: Bedfordshire, Huntingdonshire and Peterborough* (1968).

V.C.H. *Bedfordshire,* Vols. II & III (1908 & 1912) and *Huntingdonshire,* Vols. II & III (1932 & 1936).

10. Contemporary landscapes

TOWNS PLAY ONLY a minor role in the landscapes of Bedfordshire and Huntingdonshire; essentially these remain agricultural counties. Farming has gone through an important revolution since the Second World War and nowhere is there any sign of the rural distress that could have been found in the inter-war years. Then, cottage and farm stood empty and good farmland was turned over to rough pasture; now the land is used more efficiently than ever before. But this late-twentieth-century agricultural landscape can be viewed as a mixed blessing. Many have bewailed the loss of countless hedges as field has been joined to field and huge 'open' fields once more stretch across the horizon. Some have argued that most of the hedges were of little historical value as they had only been planted following the parliamentary enclosures of two hundred years ago. Unfortunately, hedgerow-removal does not discriminate between ancient and modern and it is true that many of our old boundaries, some of them unchanged for a thousand years or more, have been destroyed. What is certainly even more damaging, however, is the effect of deep ploughing and field drainage upon archaeological sites. I have mentioned earlier the disappearance of several surface features, relics of Roman settlement or medieval deserted villages, through the ploughing-up of the fields in which they lie. In common with other counties in Eastern England, Bedfordshire and Huntingdonshire now possess more arable land than at any time since the end of the thirteenth century. We are fortunate that aerial photography is now widely used as a means of identifying those sites that are no longer easily visible on the ground. As a result much has been added to the knowledge of the landscape historian. If we were merely to rely upon those pieces of evidence that can be seen on the ground then our view of the way in which the landscape has been shaped by man would be far less complete.

One aspect of the agricultural landscape that has become more important in this century, particularly in Bedfordshire, is that of market gardening and smallholdings. Most of the nineteenth-century development had been the response of individuals to market forces. The great estates, on the whole, remained aloof from such development. But in 1908 came the Smallholdings and Allotments Act that placed a duty upon the new local authorities to purchase and rent out smallholdings, with the intention of providing agricultural labourers with a proper start to a farming career. By 1915 Bedfordshire County Council had purchased and let out 2,378 acres in the market garden country around Sandy. The Duke of Bedford had set up another scheme in 1911 that concentrated upon ownership of the land rather than a permanent tenancy. A 371-acre farm at Maulden was divided into single-plot holdings of 21 acres each and purchasers were aided by generous terms of one hundred per cent mortgages with repayments spread over thirty-five years. Each plot included a farmhouse and outbuildings. Growers were recruited from around Biggleswade and the scheme brought the western part of the Lower Greensand into the field of Bedfordshire's market gardening. These small farms can still be seen in the southern half of Maulden today.

After the First World War the Land Settlement Act of 1919 saw the establishment of more smallholdings. Local authorities acquired land for rental and this time preference was given to ex-servicemen. In Bedfordshire the emphasis again fell on the established market gardening districts. Between 1919 and 1921 another 2,260 acres were purchased and divided into 660 rectangular holdings. At Sutton, for example, the sixty-acre Church Field was divided into fifty-seven plots of an acre each, the remainder being used for service roads. But these plots were less successful than the earlier ones for they were too small and lacked fencing and buildings. Tenancies were short and frequent changes led to even greater fragmentation. Quite a number of the plots were only worked on a part-time basis.

A far more successful venture was the result of an experiment in smallholdings at Potton. In the worst years of the depression between the wars P. Malcolm Stewart resolved to do something to ease the unemployment problem. He was chairman of the London Brick Company and also one of the Commissioners appointed by the Government for the Special Areas. In 1934 Stewart contributed £25,000 towards the purchase of the 535 acres of Manor Farm, Potton, with the idea that it could be worked by the unemployed to provide vegetables for the London market. Apart from Manor House, the estate consisted of Home Farm, Crossroad Farm and Spencers, together with eight cottages, most of which were in a poor condition. In 1935, before work had begun on the land, Stewart conveyed the estate to the Land Settlement Association and they invited unemployed miners from Durham to settle there. Manor House was to be a hostel for twenty-two men, who after training were to bring their families to settle in 'colonies of cottage homesteads, with newly created village greens'. Opposition came at first from local growers and those concerned about Bedfordshire's own unemployment problem, but the scheme made a successful start and new houses were built near to Crossroad Farm and along the minor road to Cockayne Hatley. The Land Settlement Association handled all the marketing of produce, but otherwise the men had a considerable degree of autonomy. In 1939, however, several of the resettled miners had to be removed from their land in order to bring the estate into full production as part of the war effort.[1] Smallholding continues in the area today and the work of the Land Settlement Association can be seen at Potton and

[1] B.R.O. CRT 130 POT 16.

also at Wyboston (see Plate 39) where a long line of standardised cottages is strung out along a private estate road to the west of the Great North Road.

Since the 1930s some changes came over the economics of market gardening. From a concentration on onions and other root crops there has been an emphasis on crops that spread labour through the year—hence a marked shift towards the planting of brussels sprouts. The sharp decline in animal manure from London also had an impact upon market gardening, and fertility levels of the soil are now maintained by chemical fertilisers. Until recently, Bedfordshire was supplying half of the country's production of brussels sprouts but lately there has been quite a dramatic decline. The crop is labour intensive and agricultural labour is becoming scarcer; at the same time growers are building more and more greenhouses and concentrating on producing early vegetables instead.

Apart from his involvement in agriculture Malcolm Stewart was also noted for his concern for the working and living conditions of his brick workers. At the time when he was involved in the Potton scheme Malcolm Stewart was also building a new village at the gates of his works at Wootton Pillinge. His father, Halley Stewart, had been the chairman of the brick firm of B. J. Forder and through amalgamation with other companies it had become the largest producer of bricks in the country, with works at Fletton and in central Bedfordshire. In 1936 the company name was changed to the London Brick Company. The new village, Stewartby, was named after the company's chairman. The settlement has grown little since its inter-war days and therefore survives as an example of planning from the 1930s. Apart from workers' homes, which were semi-detached and set well apart in large gardens, houses were provided for retired company employees together with a school, recreation area, shop, social club and neo-classical town hall. The whole development is typical of the great inter-war housing estates built on the edges of our major towns—although the facilities at Stewartby are far better— with wide avenues and large expanses of grass verge to the sweeping curves of the roads. Other than those who are still employed in the brick works there can be few who would relish living there today beneath the unbroken pall of acrid smoke from the clusters of tall chimneys around the yawning clay-pits. Yet in its time Stewartby was a marvellous improvement and excited praise from many quarters; it was even honoured with a visit by the Prince of Wales in 1934.

Another garden village, for such it was, was built in Cardington parish, just to the south of Bedford, by Short Brothers. They had established their works, making airships, in 1917, and one of the huge sheds which dominate the landscape also dates from that period, the other from 1927. It was here that the R100 and R101 were constructed and from where the latter made its fateful voyage to India, only to end in flames in France. Shortstown, the village built for the workers at the airfield, is rather less ambitious than Stewartby.

Apart from the large area given up for airship manufacture, Bedfordshire and Huntingdonshire have received an ample share of military airfields; most of them were active during the Second World War and for some years after. Fifteen airfields can be identified in the two counties; now they are mostly disused and only their concrete runways and a few buildings remain. Most of the airfields took over agricultural land; they have not greatly disrupted villages and hamlets. But at Thurleigh the airfield has swallowed the little hamlet of Whitwick Green, together with a number of interesting farmhouses. Little Staughton airfield, of which the bulk lies within Great Staughton parish, involved the demolition of half of the village of Little Staughton with Staughton Moor, including an eighteenth-century Baptist chapel and three public houses.

The railways too have declined since the 1950s; the abandoned lines now cover a greater mileage than those that remain in operation. Something of their decline has already been mentioned in Chapter Eight, but it is worth mentioning here the abandoned stations and halts. Many have been completely demolished, while others, as at Cardington, are put to some industrial purpose. Only a few have survived as domestic houses, such as the ornate station at Southill (that served the estate villages of Southill and Old Warden) on the Bedford to Hitchin line, and at Brampton. Along those lines that have been abandoned all the elements of railway furniture have gone and one wonders how much longer the Ordnance Survey will continue to mark 'Course of old railway' on its maps, particularly where the line of the former tracks has been obliterated.

The motor age that brought an end to the railways has also meant the construction of new roads and radical improvements to many others to meet the ever-increasing tide of traffic. The M1 creates an unsightly gash through south-western Bedfordshire, its solid concrete bridges a reminder that this was one of the first stretches of motorway in the country. Elsewhere, new roads have by-passed villages and small towns, particularly along the Great North Road. But villages on cross-country routes and on the A6 still suffer much from the tremendous increase in road traffic of the past two decades. The attractive centres of Ampthill and Kimbolton are ruined by the continuous flow of heavy traffic that passes through them. Not only the towns and villages are damaged by road traffic, but some of the late medieval bridges are threatened by the weight of heavy lorries that daily pass over them. Both Wansford and Huntingdon bridges have recently been relieved by by-passes, but at St Ives a single traffic flow, controlled by lights, is necessary to avoid damage to the fifteenth-century structure.

The car has also brought the commuter into Bedfordshire and Huntingdonshire and many villages are currently being transformed by the addition of large, private estates. In many places the new inhabitants have brought a renewed prosperity and helped to retain essential services, such as schools and welfare clinics. The inter-war period saw a great expansion of the suburbs of Luton and Bedford, much of it in the form of ribbon development along the main roads, as, for example, along the Old Bedford Road at Luton. Upstream from Bedford the villages of Biddenham, Clapham, Bromham and Oakley, all attractive riverside settlements, received the bulk of the new upper middle-class housing.

Settlements along the Ouse and Nene have proved particularly popular in the great post-war expansion of commuter homes, while in mid-Bedfordshire those villages close to the main railway to London with its suburban services have grown quite dramatically, especially Flitwick and Harlington. Along the riverside some villages have expanded very rapidly in recent years. Orton Longueville grew from a population of 1,256 in 1961 to 2,427 in 1971, Hemingford Grey from 1,435 to 2,309 and Oakley from 624 to 1,335. But at Little Paxton the growth over that period has been even greater, from 436 to 1,693. Yet not everywhere has experienced such dramatic increases in population. In Huntingdonshire, where London does not make its influence felt as strongly as in Bedfordshire, many villages are continuing to decline. Between 1961 and 1971 thirty-nine villages showed a decline, while forty-five measured an increase. In Bedfordshire, ninety-three places were still growing, while only twenty-nine had continued to lose population. The great majority of the losses were in northern Huntingdonshire and north-west Bedfordshire, although another pocket can be recognised on the eastern boundary of the latter county with Cambridgeshire. At Cockayne Hatley, for example, where the village has been under the control of the estate, the population fell from 122 in 1961 to 85 in 1971.

The landscape has always been subject to change. There is always the fear that the present rate of change will be more rapid and damaging than anything that has happened before. It is certainly true that our generation may be the last to see some landscape features that have been prominent for many centuries. At least we are now far more aware of what we have lost and are still losing to our technological age. Archaeological groups, local societies and national bodies abound as watch-dogs on development, although it must be admitted that none of them has a special concern for the preservation of the historical landscape *per se*. Planners too are well aware of the problems and most county authorities have a conservation unit within their planning departments, together with a full-time archaeologist. It is up to those groups not merely to record in the face of destruction but to conserve wherever possible, or else the next generation may have only the written record to tell them of man's past activity in the landscape rather than the landscape itself.

Nevertheless, it will be a long time before we reach the stage where the current landscape evolves so rapidly and dramatically that it effaces all that has gone before. In spite of technological change there is a strong sense of continuity in the countryside of Bedfordshire and Huntingdonshire. Villages stand on the same ground as their Romano-British predecessors, fields have been cultivated continuously for more than three thousand years, some roads and boundaries seem to have been determined for an even longer period. In spite of all the developments of the twentieth century, it is still true to say that to most people the upland clays of north Huntingdonshire are as remote and marginal today (albeit for different reasons) as they were when Domesday Book first recorded their settlements. The riverside villages are large and prosperous, occupying land that was settled more than three thousand years ago. The attractiveness and disadvantages of certain localities are still writ large upon the landscape. Indeed, there is an enduring quality to the physical landscape that can still explain much of the past and present patterns that man has made on the face of the two counties. As to the future, that must remain uncertain. But we must recognise that we are dealing with a man-made landscape and even that which is currently being created, no matter how undesirable or unsightly it may seem, will soon become part of that long legacy of landscape evolution. Industrial archaeologists are already preserving and romanticising objects that only a few years ago were considered ugly and not worthy of retention. One wonders how long it will be before disused airfield buildings and motorway bridges join windmills, steam-engine houses and railway stations as historic monuments in the landscapes of the two counties.

Index

Index

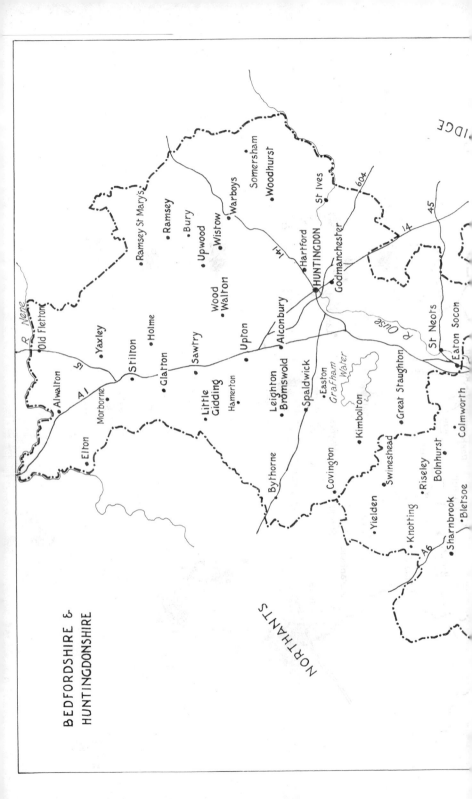

BEDFORDSHIRE &
HUNTINGDONSHIRE

NORTHANTS

R. Nene

R. Ouse

Old Fletton
Alwalton
Elton
Morborne
Yaxley
Stilton
Holme
Glatton
Sawtry
Little Gidding
Hamerton
Bythorne
Upton
Leighton Bromswold
Spaldwick
Alconbury
Wood Walton
Upwood
Wistow
Warboys
Bury
Ramsey
Ramsey St Mary's
Somersham
Woodhurst
St Ives
Hartford
HUNTINGDON
Godmanchester
Easton
Grafham Water
Kimbolton
Covington
Yielden
Knotting
Sharnbrook
Swineshead
Riseley
Bolnhurst
Bletsoe
Great Staughton
St Neots
Eaton Socon
Colmworth

A1
B5
A6
14
45
604
141

BRIDGE